Now that your company has downsized,
restructured and reengineered,

How's All the Work Going to Get Done?

By
Don Blohowiak

CAREER
PRESS

Franklin Lakes, NJ

Copyright © 1995 by Don Blohowiak

HOW'S ALL THE WORK GOING TO GET DONE?
ISBN 1-56414-192-6, $21.99
Cover design by The Gottry Communications Group, Inc.
Printed in the U.S.A. by Book-mart Press

To order this title by mail, please include price as noted above, $2.50 handling per order, and $1.00 for each book ordered. Send to: Career Press, Inc., 3 Tice Road, P.O. Box 687, Franklin Lakes, NJ 07417.

Or call toll-free 1-800-CAREER-1 (N.J. and Canada: 201-848-0310) to order using VISA or MasterCard, or for further information on books from Career Press.

Library of Congress Cataloging-in-Publication Data

Blohowiak, Donald W.
    How is all the work going to get done? / by Don Blohowiak.
       p.   cm.
    Includes index.
    ISBN 1-56414-192-6
    1. Manpower planning. 2. Labor productivity. 3. Compensation management. 4. Organizational change. I. Title. II. Title: Now that your company has downsized, restructured, and reengineered
HF5549.5.M3B56 1995
658.3'14--dc20   95-24871
                                                CIP

For Ben and Aaron,
for whom my pride
is exceeded only by my love

Contents

Preface

As the dark waters of organizational turmoil at my workplace swirled around me, their forces pushed my career steadily upward. Through no plotting or lobbying on my part, my functional responsibilities, the number of employees reporting to me and my income have all increased—as the number of my peers around me decreased.

At the same time, my sick days have ticked upward since my firm's first high-stress restructuring kicked off. In prior—more tranquil—times, I'd gone for years without suffering so much as a sniffle. But since catching the chill of my company's first downsizing, my consumption of over-the-counter medications and the number of days I spend nursing a passing malady have gone from zero to something more than that.

I wrote this book in the midst of my employer's third attempt to trim another double-digit percentage from the payroll—following reengineering efforts in the previous 18 months that felled fully 40 percent of our full-time employees. All while remaining exceptionally profitable and improving customer satisfaction.

You might wonder, is it really possible to raise morale, productivity and quality in a workplace seized by post-downsizing shock waves?

Yes. It is possible after enduring "Radical Change"—the turmoil commonly known as downsizing, restructuring or reengineering—to lead your staff to do things they didn't know they could do before going through it. This book is a collection of techniques and behaviors that you personally can use after the downsizing, no matter what your position in your newly flattened organization, to help your staff work smarter, harder and happier.

In wrestling with organizational restructuring, your physical endurance, mental agility and spiritual constitution all face exhausting trials. The action-packed days and work-filled nights ahead may well become the most taxing—and most rewarding—days of your career. Enjoy the adventure! And please let me know how you fare.

Don Blohowiak
Box 791
Princeton Junction, NJ 08550-0791
Internet: 76016.1446@compuserve.com

Introduction

"There is nothing more difficult to take in hand, more perilous to conduct, or more uncertain in its success than to take the lead in the introduction of a new order of things."
— Niccolò Machiavelli

If you feel the need to read this book, your organization is asking (or demanding) more from you and your staff than you believe you can reasonably deliver. Worse, if your organization has undergone a Radical Change, you know that it is capable of eliminating your position in an instant no matter how hard you work or how well you perform. You're afraid for your own livelihood, and your shell-shocked staff (what remains of it) is looking to you for assurance, guidance and some magic you just don't have. The challenge of leadership—and the value of steady employment—have taken on a whole new meaning.

Nothing in this book can promise you secure employment. (And as the Conclusion makes clear, independent wealth is about the only security there is.) Still, you should find this book hopeful as well as helpful. It makes an honest assessment of the tumult in today's turbulent workplace and offers you many

YOU DRAW YOUR LIVELIHOOD, NOT YOUR *LIVING*, FROM YOUR EMPLOYER. THERE ARE NO PRIZES FOR KILLING YOURSELF AT YOUR DESK.

ways to think about and approach organizational life as an overburdened manager.

Like a stranger in your own workplace

Given the experiences that led you to seek this book, you may feel bitterly betrayed by your once benevolent employer. You may have witnessed a callousness on the part of your superiors of which you did not think they were capable. You may have been forced to trade the incomes of long-time friends and colleagues for this quarter's profits. Your loyalty may have broken into angry apathy. Your desk probably is buried under a hopelessly heaping mound of work that never shrinks and only grows. The atmosphere in your workplace may have deteriorated from pleasant and professional to confused and chaotic. Every day you may find yourself confronting only three kinds of problems: crises, emergencies and disasters. You've likely suffered staff, budget and program cuts. With the popular trend to outsourcing, you may feel considerably diminished—more like a specialized purchasing agent than an effective manager. While you know the concept of lifetime employment is mere fantasy, you're not sure you'll stay on the payroll even through the month.

Whether you've faced this environment for years or days, there's help between these covers. Everything in this book is grounded in reality without abstractions, wishful thinking or magical incantations. On these pages, you'll find frank talk, real-life Radical Change experiences and an honest perspective. This book addresses the knotty issues confronting you as a manager in the workplace revolution. It offers help for each of your important roles: as a steward of the organization that pays your salary, as a leader to those for whose work you've been given responsibility and as a vulnerable human being in a time of great stress. Let's address these roles for a brief moment. Despite your career aspirations, your deep dedication to your employer and all the creativity, energy and commitment you've surrendered to the organization whose name appears on all your paychecks, you draw your livelihood, not your *living*, from your employer. You have a job, perhaps a great job, but it's only a job—a vehicle by which you earn money. There are millions of jobs (most of them about as much fun as yours right now). Your job is important, but the fate of the world does not depend on it, and you could always find another.

Your employer has a right to expect great work and results from you, but no one (at least no one for whom you'll be able to work for very long) should expect you to do the impossible. You must draw and manage appropriate boundaries. There are no prizes for killing yourself at your desk. Here's an important truth you're unlikely to hear from your boss or from many motivational speakers: You cannot do it all. In organizations that have suffered a bout of Radical Change, the expectations for most managers are simply unreasonable.

Yet, by making smart choices, setting the right priorities, getting your staff out of their emotional slump and working on high-value activities, you can still produce great results and keep your good health.

Short Take: Don't just do something!

An organization buffeted by wrenching technological, economic or social changes faces a terrible period of adjustment as it struggles to adapt. Radically modifying internal operations to contend with the topsy-turvy external environment can be a horrendously long, consuming and painful process. In such agonizing circumstances, one may feel incapable of taking on the immense, mind-numbing problems that confront the organization. It's easy to become focused on something other than all the massive and increasingly familiar problems. Executives paralyzed by an overwhelming agenda of insolubles often turn to holding many meetings, issuing many memos and engaging in activities about as useful as polishing the brass of a ship sinking deep into dark waters.

Task-oriented people seem compelled to fulfill an irrepressible urge to do something, take charge of a matter and see it through to completion. That relentless drive to accomplish only focuses energy on the irrelevant or the insignificant, which are attractive because they're easy to influence. So, while a company teeters at the financial precipice with declining sales and raging expenses, the sales executive is test-driving possible new fleet car models instead of finding out why customers are defecting. Meanwhile, her colleague, the chief financial officer, toils to design nothing more substantial than a new travel expense report form.

If you're confronting daunting circumstances, keep perspective to keep from being overwhelmed. Doing the hard, important work may seem endlessly unrewarding and feel like you're accomplishing nothing. What's more, the most important and valuable work you need to do may not be very visible or instantly effective as it slowly chips away at your organization's enormous and complex challenges. Stay focused and working on things that matter, even though it's much more seductive to complete things that don't.

Outlook: Mostly cloudy is partly sunny

"The lowest ebb is the turn of the tide," wrote Henry Wadsworth Longfellow. Things probably do look bleak or at least a lot less encouraging than you've seen before. The notion of work as fun is a faded fad. The environment you're now working in may not be ideal, but it probably beats the alternative of unemployment. (Still, as several outplaced former colleagues of mine have pointed out, there is life after any given employer.) Chapter 10 details many personal survival skills you can use during this endurance contest you face daily. One worth mentioning here is the concept of resume-quality work.

In the extensive challenges thrown your way by Radical Change, you will be afforded numerous occasions to take on new responsibilities, to solve new problems and to grapple with new opportunities. These are all circumstances you likely would not have faced (or certainly not in the same number and frequency) in the old, familiar, steady-as-she-goes work world so long past. These challenges give you a chance to not only help your employer, but also yourself. Look, your employment could end tomorrow (literally, with no warning), but they can only fire you once. If that event presents itself, it may well be out of your control (or even your boss's). So while you can't insulate yourself from the possibility, you shouldn't fret over it either. In fact, prudence suggests that you should prepare yourself for the possibility; give thought to the course of action you'd take if your boss makes an unexpected pilgrimage to your office to begin a discussion of your career options.

If your workload has increased because your employer indiscriminately cut staff without a clear vision for a better functioning, more successful organization in the future, you should begin contemplating your move to another employer. It's highly likely you're going to need to find a new source of income sooner rather than later. Lightening an organization's short-term financial load by eliminating employees

WHAT WAS IS GONE. AND IT'S NOT COMING BACK. THE TASK NOW IS TO CREATE THE FUTURE.

13

is like cutting off one's hands to lose weight. A poorly managed organization that downsizes to cut costs simply devolves into a more anemic, more poorly managed firm. Similarly, beware of an organization that turns over its people to deploy the Count Dracula Strategy: Let's get some fresh blood into the organization (with, one hopes, some new ideas unconstrained by the organization's past!). The unspoken trade-off: purging competency, continuity and the corporation's history and mission.

In any event, you should prepare yourself for the possibility that your current post will yield to another. Do this by becoming fully engaged in your new, exhausting role, learning as much as you can and getting as much from it as possible. That way, if things don't work out where you're currently employed, you can offer a new employer (perhaps yourself) a whole armory of skills and experience you wouldn't otherwise have obtained working in the bygone era of Business as Usual.

In this context, the very trying days ahead are as formative as they are fatiguing. You'll build not only character but marketable skills that will serve to your advantage even if your immediate employer doesn't fully appreciate them. The worst and the best of your career lies straight ahead. I hope that you find this book a worthy companion and able assistant on your journey.

Part 1

Responding to the big bang of Radical Change

Chapter 1

In the immediate aftermath of Radical Change

Your old familiar organization ceased to exist when it underwent the Radical Change of downsizing, restructuring or reengineering. In its new state, it isn't just a different version of Old Familiar, Inc. with merely fewer workers or different work processes. Old Familiar, Inc.—the company that hired you, trained you, steadily increased your standard of living, showered you with ever-richer benefits, promised you a lifelong career path in exchange for diligent work—was wiped from the face of the earth by the blast of Radical Change.

The new, leaner, meaner organization that replaces Old Familiar, Inc. has a different purpose, a new way of operating and unfamiliar conventions with which it deals with your work and your life. Not only has your employer changed completely, but the very society it represents—the one in which you and your staff were productive members and felt so comfortable—has also changed forever. Without leaving the payroll, you've become a stranger in a strange land with rules that change daily, where status is won

IF YOU CAN'T LET GO OF THE PAST, LEAVE WITH IT. RESIGN.

and lost for no apparent reason, where justice seems not an inalienable right but a gross inconvenience to assuring quarterly profits.

Facing the demons of change

As a survivor of the restructured workplace, you may feel as though you have blood on your hands, having forcibly separated good people from their livelihoods, their friends and colleagues and the society in which they were contributing members. You may be racked by guilt, even though you understand that what you did was for the good of the corporate body and that the needs of the many exceed the needs of the few. You may be emotionally drained, exhausted from the secret planning, the anguishing decisions and the ugly deeds you were called on to execute. Even if you didn't actually have to fire anyone but had a hand in planning (or just advanced knowledge of) the Radical Change, you're probably tired from the Burden of Knowing— secretly carrying around information with serious impact on your colleagues.

Now that the purge is behind you, you probably have additional responsibilities with new functions and new people reporting to you (either because you inherited other departments that previously reported to a now-departed boss, or because eliminating layers of management has caused more people in your own corner of the organization to report directly to you). You may feel overwhelmed at first.

Good! At least you have no delusions about the immensity of the task before you.

You know that the transformation was born of pain. You may feel a gnawing sense of failure because you—despite your hard work—were unable to prevent Old Familiar, Inc. from deteriorating into the unfamiliar and undesirable place it has just become. Take heart. You cannot blame yourself for not preventing the change or for having survived it while other good people were tossed off the payroll with little or no dignity.

No matter your role in bringing it about, you'll have an attitude about the Radical Change. If you helped to shape the change or you've wholly bought into it, you may be one of its champions. If you had little or no input into the change, you might think of yourself as an unwitting participant (or even victim) of it, while your staff might see you as one of the persecutors. You might consider yourself more of a Missourian: "Show me this makes sense." If you disagree with the thinking behind the change or the way it was executed, you might count yourself among the cynics. If you are in either of the last two categories, consider yourself a member of the loyal (and publicly silent) opposition.

Whatever category you find yourself in, you must recognize your attitude toward the Radical Change and reconcile your feelings about it. Letting go of the security, comfort and certainty of the organization you knew and loved is jarring and flat-out frightening. But it need not be debilitating. As a manager, you are a person of responsibility in this

SURVIVING
EMPLOYEES GET AN
INCREASED WORK
LOAD, MAYBE FACE
A DEMOTION AND
SUFFER AT LEAST
DASHED HOPES FOR
ANY PROMOTION IN
THE NEAR FUTURE.

new, unstable society, and your charge is to make it into something that works. As long as you draw a check from—and hold a position of responsibility in—this strangely changed organization, you owe it your best work. Judging, blaming and wondering "what if" won't undo what's been done. You must now focus on what you're going to do about it. Amidst all the disappointments and uncertainties, focus on one positive: You can help create whatever this new entity is going to be, lending your best thinking to shape its identity, standards and successes.

In the real world, old, outdated buildings are torn down to make way for newer, more modern ones. In the business world, organizations must destroy themselves before they can rebuild.

If you can't embrace the future or let go of the past, leave with it. Resign. If you're determined to stay put, then make the most of it. You'll never achieve greatness in meeting these new challenges if you're paralyzed by hostility, frustration or fear. Confront and conquer your anger, self-doubt and fear of failure. You owe it to yourself and all the people who look to you for leadership—in the context of stability, confidence and a willingness to confront the unknown—to reach deep inside to find the courage, the will and the open-mindedness to stalk and stare this new monster in the face. And then make peace with it.

Short Take: An organization is not a family!

One of the reasons the undoing of Old Familiar, Inc. is so unsettling for employees is that many people have come to think of their employer as a kind of extended family. People remaining on the payroll just watched their corporate parent coldly throw out fellow family members. The house rules they've mastered to please the organizational parent are suddenly invalidated, leaving some to feel about as secure as a stranded child. Senior management, previously seen as a benevolent provider, has suddenly turned into a mean and dysfunctional authority figure.

No business or organization is a family. But some companies say they are, and many others have for decades implied that they are. Following World War II, most large businesses enjoyed the Presumption of Consumption, whereby somebody somewhere was virtually certain to buy whatever they produced. In the profitable good old days, many businesses fostered a feeling of paternalism in their organizations. Employees were well cared for by their benevolent provider. Maybe it wasn't quite love, but it was close—with steady and healthy raises to the base salary, generous vacation and sick day allowances, paid health and life insurance, paid education, company-funded sports teams and benefit upon employer-paid benefit. All this sweetened the implied assurance of employment through retirement in many major corporations and institutions. No wonder people began to confuse their organization with their family: The employer as a surrogate parent was perhaps more civil, generous and nurturing than the real thing!

Some companies still proclaim in their ads and in other corporate communications that they are, through some kind of strange alchemy, a family. However, business economics today make it virtually impossible for an organization to act like a family or extend to its employees unconditional love in the form of guaranteed employment and ever-richer benefits.

This might not be so bad. Business-as-family implies a promise of unconditionally accepting even nonproductive employees. The attitude of "we're a family here" works subconsciously to discourage managers from firing nonperformers. At the same time, managers hiring a "family" may tend to populate a homogenous employee base by engaging in antidiversity hiring practices.

Organizations in today's new economic order will become less and less like social institutions and more and more like task-centered networks of craftsmen. In this new scheme, skilled people deliver specific services on an *ad hoc* basis to achieve an objective (much like subcontractors build a house and software consultants provide skills for hire on given projects). This may become a familiar model you will grow to love.

21

Mourning in the morning: Meet your post-restructuring staff

If your organization just underwent a Radical Change that eliminated many jobs, or you know it is about to (whether for the first time or the tenth), here are some suggestions for facing the "survivors" immediately following the purge. If your job is to break news of the Radical Change to your employees, address the Five W's: What's happening, When and Where it's happening, Who it affects and Why it's happening. The most important question for you to address, the one foremost on each employee's mind, is simply: What does all this mean to me?

As soon as possible, gather your new staff (what remains of your old one and the people you've just inherited). Expect to encounter a wide spectrum of emotion. The pain of downsizing dredges up insecurities and emotions that employees may have had lurking under their normal, stable-on-the-job exteriors. Panic, frustration and depression may well be staring you in the face on the fateful "morning after." Some surviving employees will experience grief and depression. Decades-long associations with co-workers may have been terminated in an instant (one of my colleagues described the downsizing experience as a "corporate Passover" in which "blood marks victims' office doors"). Life as employees knew it is dead. Despite official memos full of optimistic corporatespeak, these employees imagine a horrible, tortured future in which they're forced to toil like indentured servants only to have their own livelihoods suddenly stripped from them in the dark of night.

Because there was probably little or no warning before the Radical Change snapped its jaws, people have not prepared for this. And even with ample warning, they may still lack the skills necessary to cope with either the emotional fallout or the professional demands they now face. These people need you to provide competent, sensitive leadership to help them through this traumatic experience. As one of my staff put it, "We need emotional stability more than pencils, staples or computers."

The unlucky "survivors"

Many, even most, of your employees may feel they are not the lucky ones just because they're still with what remains of Old Familiar, Inc. "The ones who left are getting more from the company than I am," they may reason. After all, those departing the company may have left with some combination of severance, enhanced pension, financial and career counseling and maybe even time to travel or relax. In contrast, surviving employees get an increased workload, maybe face a demotion and suffer at least dashed hopes for any promotion in the near future. About all they can look forward to—in addition to picking up the slack left by their departed comrades—is flat or reduced pay and the constant, haunting fear of getting cut in the next round of restructuring.

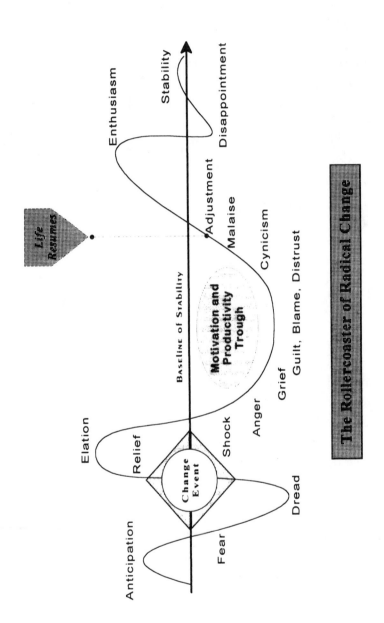

The Rollercoaster of Radical Change

Short Take: Morbid metaphors surround downsizing

When people speak of trimming employees from an organization's payroll, their language betrays their true view of what many try to portray as a clinical process. It is no longer fashionable in formal conversation to speak of "firing" people or even "laying them off" or giving them "pink slips" (aren't those for phone messages?). Formal corporatespeak prefers contorted euphemisms for dismissing employees, such as "streamlining," "outplacing," "rightsizing" or "making reductions in force." Informal speech, however, yields a very different vocabulary.

In the vernacular, even "firing" is too euphemistic. People speak of losing their co-workers in much more graphic and repugnant terms: "purges," "bloodletting," "assassinations," "holocausts," "executions," "massacres" and "slash-and-burn." Workers slated for dismissal are said to be "getting the kiss of death," "axed," "nuked," "shot at dawn," "taken out," "getting the bullet" or "blown away." People remaining after the dismissals are "survivors."

Using such intense words to describe separating someone from his or her employer speaks volumes about how very important, how central to our lives, work really is.

When it comes to downsizing (even staff reductions due to the most well-planned reengineering efforts), management claims of running the operation "leaner and meaner" amount to absolute truth in advertising. As the headline in an ad for *Fortune* magazine put it, "What's worse, getting laid off on Friday or being told to pick up the slack on Monday?"

Conscientious employees may vent deeply felt anger and ask such heartfelt questions as, "Why didn't anyone do the planning to avoid this?", "Don't they (senior management) care about employees anymore?", "How do they think all this work is going to get done?" and "How can we concentrate on quality work when all we can think about is how scared we are?". Following an inevitably messy and stressful downsizing, the victims who remain employed in the organization are far more likely to view the event as "dumbsizing" than "rightsizing."

Misery, mission and meaning: Communicate until it hurts

Honest, straightforward communication from you to your staff is the best antidote to the poisonous environment that naturally erupts from a downsizing—whatever the cause. Acknowledge that you understand your employees' feelings of loss, fear, anger and guilt; their feelings are normal and a compliment to their humanity (not a sign of denying "the new reality"). As one senior manager told me, "I'm getting used to the idea that people, even top executives, are going to be let go on a moment's notice. What I can't get used to is the expectation that we're not supposed to feel anything when they are."

Talking about emotions in the workplace may seem unbusinesslike. It might also seem unnecessary, especially if a great deal of information preceded the event. But acknowledged or not, the emotions exist. If left to fester, negative emotions can significantly affect a person's performance, just as a pebble in your shoe can escalate from being annoying to actually impeding you.

Your primary objective is to instill confidence in your group—even if senior management's direction for steering the organization isn't popular or perfectly clear. If you can, calmly restate the factors that led to the company's painful decision to curse itself with this wretched series of events. Above all, be credible. Gilding horse manure doesn't change its essential nature. Some senior manager may implore you to bolster morale, to put the approved spin on ugly events. While you shouldn't work against your employer, you must understand that your charges will look to you for integrity. They'll repay you with earnest work even with no sign of light at the end of the organizational tunnel, because they see the glow of integrity shining in your corner of the firm.

If the Radical Change brings with it new policies (stated or implied) about how the organization views its obligations to employees, be honest about that. The truth may not be pleasant, but it is what it is, and your employees have a right to know where they stand.

Where you reasonably can, accentuate the positive; make a case for a future better than the present, one shaped by everyone still with the firm. Unless the company made the changes based on patently insane reasoning, there should be cause for hope for a more stable environment in the future.

One way I tried to lift the confidence of my group immediately following a restructuring was to have everyone gather in a conference room for a brief meeting. After acknowledging the difficult period leading up to the restructuring, I spoke of my genuine expectation for brighter days ahead and how I was depending on everyone in the room to deliver his or her best work—and best thinking—to continually reinvent the organization in the face of an ever-changing environment.

"I'm excited about working with you," I told them. Because of the way the restructuring at our company had been designed, I had handpicked everyone in that room, and I told them so. I proudly

ALL PLANS WORK IN THEORY. THEORIES DON'T GET THE WORK DONE.

27

said, "With no reservations, I'm betting my career on you. Working together, we're going to do great work, achieve great things. We all have something to look forward to here. It's our future. We can't be entirely certain of exactly how it will unfold, but we certainly can make the most of it. Because we can't do things the way we've always done them, we have an opportunity to do things in ways we've never done them before. That offers each of us an exciting opportunity to grow, to try new things and develop new skills and competencies to enhance our careers."

Ongoing communication

During this delicate time, use face-to-face discussion—not e-mail, voice mail or memos—to manage your people. (During the early, dark hours of our restructuring, I handed out rolls of Lifesavers® candies to my staff with a note attached urging them, "Hang in there!") Your human touch must balance corporate management's more sterile, formal pronouncements. Senior management memos on major change are often edited by committee and professional spin doctors; they're sanitized and carefully constructed to be noncommittal or (often, it seems) unclear.

Even when memos communicate clearly, not every employee reads every one of them. I've attended many a meeting in which the discussion centered on some apparent confusion by the work force over a new policy. Stymied senior managers would retort with great indignation, "We mentioned that in a memo!" Well, not everyone reads every word of corporate gospel, and even if they did, they might not understand, recall or believe what they read. Person-to-person contact gives employees the opportunity to ask specific questions and clarify in their own minds conflicting or confusing information. It gives you an opportunity to reinforce key themes.

In the intense period immediately following a restructuring, you can't communicate enough. Your employees are starving for details that can help them understand what the Radical Change means to them. In the absence of clear, detailed information from management, people fill the void by sharing gossip with total disregard for accuracy (never spoil a good story with the truth!). Desperate for answers that no one really has, employees will waste immeasurable time trading speculation, interpretation and misinformation. The ratio of negative conjecturing to positive will run at least 10 to 1. Especially intriguing plots, even far-fetched ones, might catch fire like parched prairie grass in August. The more frequently a juicy piece of gossip is repeated, the more credibility it seems to carry.

While you may not be any more informed than your employees, don't add fuel to the fire by joining the flights-of-fancy frenzy. If you even casually entertain with your staff any musings about what might happen next in the organizational saga, you lend credibility to the tall tales contest.

If it's appropriate, rally enthusiasm for the organization's next chapter with an appropriate rallying cry. When my employer underwent its major re-structuring, our Radical Change was designed to correct a politicized, divided and insularly-focused organization that had evolved during a century of operating. To introduce the new organization and its new business model to our sales force, we held a large kickoff meeting. I coined this phrase as the meeting theme: "One Team Putting Customers First." It crystallized the essence of our metamorphosis from a house divided and removed from the market to one united to serve it. The phrase immediately caught on across the organization because it reflected the aspirations and commitment of the employees in the newly incarnated organization, and it still emblazons companywide employee communications two years after that sales meeting.

YOUR PRIMARY OBJECTIVE IS TO INSTILL CONFIDENCE IN YOUR GROUP.

A rallying cry can serve as a constant and inspiring reminder of the organization's new mission. It can also fall flat on its face and be counterproductive if it's off the mark. Case in point: At an employee meeting at a manufacturer that recently underwent a Radical Change, workers complained that some newly reengineered processes weren't working as planned, making it difficult to deliver quality output. The rallying cry repeated by executives responding to the complaints did little to inspire the troops. "It doesn't matter!" chanted the vice presidents. What they meant by that retort was that internal short-comings should not stand in the way of delivering quality to customers—that employees had an obligation to work around the systems. Somehow, the positive and inspiring part of the message was lost in translation. "It doesn't matter" was taken as being insensitive and unresponsive. Within hours, echoes of the phrase—and not the logic behind it—reverberated throughout the company's offices. Angry employees repeated it for weeks with disgust as a sign of senior management's insensitivity and isolation from operating concerns. Perhaps if those well-intending executives had chanted, "Do whatever it takes to get it right!", the point would have been clearer.

Pruning the grapevine

Be aware of what people are conjecturing and address real concerns. Talk to your employees individually. Ask directly, "What's hot on the grapevine?" If your group is large or far-flung, consider using brief, formal surveys to gauge employees' concerns so you can address them. After uncovering the rumors, consider publicly debunking them by holding a meeting or publishing a memo in which you list rumors and then follow the litany with statements of fact.

Taking the time or paying a consultant to catalog what's distracting your employees will be repaid many times over in the productivity gains that result from reducing the time people spend worrying, conjecturing and gossiping. Another advantage in polling your work force is the opportunity to gain relevant insights into the Radical Change that management failed to have, no matter how thorough its planning. Pass along to your superiors these unexpected insights. Raising such issues at this point in the process gives management a chance to correct course earlier in the journey, saving time, anguish and money.

About face!

The Radical Change came about because today's topsy-turvy business world forced your organization to turn its standard operating procedures inside out. Before, during and after the planning for the Radical Change, the economic world continued to spin wildly off its long-familiar axis. It continues to twist in unpredictable revolutions. That means today's Radical Change will be superseded and countermanded by tomorrow's Radical Change. Whenever the dust seems to settle, a new, unexpected aftershock kicks it up again.

This is true in every organization. In today's change-by-the-minute world, there are no safe harbors—a bitter and shocking lesson to many in traditionally insulated sectors of the economy, such as insurance, health care and government. Prepare yourself and your employees to accept and cope with this uncomfortable but inevitable reality.

Rising to the occasion: slavish days and work-filled nights

When Radical Change sweeps through your organization, it presents itself with all the force and sensitivity of a tornado. Slightly (or more so) fearful of your own security in the organization, you work like never before. You may find yourself being consumed with the process of change instead of productively running the business. Many consultants brought in to aid the transition will, likewise, be consumed with process. Meetings related to managing the process will be scheduled for days instead of minutes.

Radical Change events can consume most of your workday as you incorporate changes in organizational direction, attend endless meetings and try to deal with the professional and emotional needs of your confused and frightened staff. Keeping up with all of that and the work that needs to be done makes for an endless marathon punctuated by hard sprints. Monitor your activities so that you are driving the process more than being driven by it. That means, foremost, maintaining your health and sanity and keeping a sense of perspective (see Chapter 10). It means identifying and filling the most important vacuums created by the Radical Change (see Chapter 6).

While it's easy to dwell on the negative fallout of Radical Change, take a moment now and then with your crew to celebrate your successes. Amidst the nonstop challenges, you're going to score some victories. Stand and applaud, salute your people, slap some backs and shake some hands. That's the way you'll all find the energy and commitment to keep going forward through the endless stream of chest-deep mud left in the wake of Radical Change.

Embrace the change; see the opportunities it presents. "If there is any period one would desire to be born in," asked Ralph Waldo Emerson, "is it not the age of Revolution; when the old and the new stand side by side, and admit of being compared; when the energies of all men are searched by fear and by hope; when the historic glories of the old can be compensated by the rich possibilities of the new era?"

This "new era" provides you with a chance to develop and demonstrate leadership as few others have. It offers you the perfect platform to stretch and to use skills you never had the opportunity to use and maybe didn't know you had. Viewed in the right light, this strange turn of events is a wonderful and welcome character- and career-builder. It's a chance to strut your stuff and make a difference in ways you may never have thought possible.

Chapter 2

Precarious promises, imperfect processes and impromptu performance

When the switch was thrown to crank up your organization's newly designed structure or its recently reengineered processes, it most likely followed months of planning, rumors and anticipation (a mix of hope and fear).

Surprise! The Grand Plan may have a few holes

When the old finally gave way to the new, some things probably didn't work very well or at all. Almost invariably, major redesign plans overestimate the speed at which changes can be made and underestimate difficulties in implementing them. A fix expected to be effective in three months may take more than a year to work operationally and longer to pay off financially.

PEOPLE DON'T PERFORM TO FOUR DECIMAL PLACES.

Five flaws often accompany the grand debut of a Radical Change based on a not-so-Grand Plan.

1. The Radical Change ignores the past. Despite the many hours of thinking, debating and plotting, the restructuring architects who drew the new blueprint probably gave insufficient—if any— attention to the thinking of the people truly responsible for running the operation. Consultants planning a newfangled procedure to speed up parts-painting tend to spend too much time with the head of manufacturing and not enough time with the people who paint the parts. Then, when the new payoffs fail to materialize, you hear few gasps of surprise from people close to the work, but you hear the resounding cry, "Why didn't they talk to us first?" Those "good on paper" solutions were left to be implemented by people who had little or no input into them. They don't believe, don't understand and don't want to change. And your job is to lead them to the new destination by blazing the trail along the newly designed route.

2. The Radical Change rehashes the past. Some "reinvention" of work is no more profound than moving your furniture from one room to another. You spend lots of time and work up a sweat, but fundamentally not much changes. Here are some ways organizations shuffle furniture:

- Modestly improving the automation of procedures.
- Changing personnel or reporting structures without changing basic workflow.

- Forcing employees to sit through flashy but hollow training programs fashioned on the latest hot-sounding management concept.

These and other imitations of reinvention may tweak short-term results while major gains remain elusive. Hastily planned overhauls—in response to a sales downturn, a need for higher margins or an attempt to be fashionable—may yield results ranging from ineffective to disastrous.

One common version of "rehash reengineering" might be called the Move the Work Across the Hall deception. In this scenario, the organization doesn't really do less or different work, but each department tries to punt away some task it used to do to you and other unsuspecting folks. The mailroom becomes more efficient by no longer separating your mail from your colleagues' mail or opening incoming envelopes. Instead, it shifts the burden of separating and opening department mail to the fewer and already heavily burdened secretaries (if any are left) or to their bosses. The HR department becomes more efficient by moving record-keeping responsibilities to you and other overworked, highly stressed line managers. The accounting department increases its productivity by requiring others to audit invoices for mathematical accuracy.

Shuffling work from one desk to many others often means transferring it to people whose time is much more valuable and much more expensive than that of the people who gave the work away in order to become more efficient or whose positions were eliminated in the name of productivity. This charade may not be exposed until even *more* consultants conduct a new round of process analysis. In the meantime, actual productivity invisibly slides downward because of new procedures intended to boost it.

3. The Radical Change projects an unlikely future. Great expectations for savings in labor or materials may have been pegged to unrealistic levels of human productivity, untested equipment or processes that flow flawlessly only on paper. People don't perform to four decimal places, and ivory-tower planners can easily overlook some operational detail that later will appear glaringly obvious. New machine-based systems, whether mechanized or computerized, often fail to deliver at peak capacity before maddening little problems present themselves and resist all reasonable efforts to be corrected.

In rushing to grab the projected gains from the new process, the proponents of change may provide inadequate testing or none at all before unleashing the new and burying the old. The gains do not materialize. Worse, hard-dollar costs may actually escalate due to substandard production (wasted materials, forced overtime), missed deadlines (postponed sales revenues, disappointed and even lost customers) and process fixes (more investment, more consulting fees). Soft costs escalate, too, as employee, investor and customer confidence in management erodes.

ALMOST INVARIABLY, MAJOR REDESIGN PLANS OVERESTIMATE THE SPEED AT WHICH CHANGES CAN BE MADE AND UNDERESTIMATE DIFFICULTIES IN IMPLEMENTING THEM.

What counts is not just the ability to imagine a better future, but the capability to implement one.

4. The Radical Change is based on cutting costs. Slashing positions, adopting new technology or designing intricate changes in process are often justified by great expectations for savings in operating costs. Trimming expenses is only half the reasoning that should lead to the pain of undertaking a Radical Change. The other half is improving services: designing the changes so they result in improved customer satisfaction (a better, more valuable product, faster delivery, better response time, etc.). Without this fundamental undergirding to support the change, the organization invites a major breakdown for two simple reasons. First, the thorough but incomplete planning may overstate the savings (or worse, the changes may carry hidden costs of implementation that result in increased expenses); second, the turmoil and confusion that naturally accompany Radical Change inevitably result in degrading service to customers, who may in turn retaliate by doing less business in the future. So with one critical oversight, the enterprise instantly builds two on-ramps to the Disaster Expressway: failing to get expected cost savings and even increasing costs, and alienating customers, causing revenues to fall (perhaps forever).

5. The Radical Change ignores the "human factor." Redesigning a process or corporate structure involves more than flow charts and process diagrams. It involves humanity: habits, insecurities, misunderstandings. Announcing and implementing a redesigned organization or work process does not mean you've changed either management or employee behavior (see Chapter 6). Endless flow charts, edicts from top management and sloganeering won't effect change one bit until people adopt the new system or organization while actually changing how they personally do their jobs. An organization produces work through a collection of actions by individuals at every level. That's true no matter how many machines also do some of the work and despite whatever management philosophy the company's top officers claim in the annual report as guiding company performance.

Consulting on massive change is easier than implementing it

To say that organizational planning is an academic exercise is usually correct: If your organization pinned its future to a scheme devised by a big-name management consulting firm, the Grand Plan was probably devised by people (often very young people) who distinguished themselves in a purely academic environment. They got good grades at good universities. They can draw charts, make overheads and create buzzwords with amazing alacrity. Do these skills qualify them to create practical solutions? Would you bet your business on such whippersnappers? Trying to divine why so many top executives do count on these people is beyond the scope of this book. Regardless of the shots one might level at the young, high-priced consultants (freshly minted MBAs can start near six figures) whose obvious intelligence far exceeds their business experience, your senior management bet many dollars and much time and credibility on the change process it expects the consultants to produce. Top management will pay attention to the advice. And this sets up some natural tension between the guests and those who toil for the hosts.

The tail that wags you

Some organizational cultures routinely reject ideas if they are "not invented here." This behavior is commonly referred to as NIH syndrome. When outside consultants are suddenly injected into the corporate organism in a desperate attempt to save it from itself, a reverse NIH syndrome may manifest itself. Ideas and suggestions that you and your staff offer to senior management may suddenly carry little or no weight when balanced against those from consultants.

The consultants' charge from the top sometimes carries a mandate nothing short of "save the company." That can translate to an unspoken but unmistakable attitude that says: "Even though I'm an outsider, I have power that you as an employee responsible for this area do not have. I can ask for and get information you cannot. I can recommend changes without consulting you, perhaps without ever speaking to you. If you don't like it, complain to the president. And good luck, pal, because even if you've got the guts to complain, I'll have the president's ear many times before and after your petty whining distracts her from this important mission."

Not all consulting assignments result in "us versus them." But to many line employees and managers, being surrounded by empowered consultants feels like a hostile takeover. "They forget who is working for who," laments an acquaintance of mine about the consultants swarming around her. "Aren't we the customer here?" she asks. "The tail is wagging the dog."

Enabled dependency

Prolonged exposure to jargon-spewing consultants and their convoluted process analysis charts, sophisticated regression analysis and impossibly complex modeling formulae can lead senior executives to develop a malady one might describe as Consultant Dependency. This condition is marked by their unspoken but powerful condemnation of everyone outside the highest inner circle: "None of the people on our payroll ever produced anything this dazzling. Heck, most of 'em aren't even smart enough to understand stuff this intricate (especially since I'm not sure I understand it). Better not waste our time muddying the waters with input from the schlubs we employ—not when it's all we can do to interpret the nearly unintelligible, and therefore brilliant, reports, graphs and buzzwords of those expensive consultants!"

Before long, top management stops seeking input from its staff, even its senior staff. *After all, the reasoning seems to go, aren't they the folks who got us into this mess? If they really knew what needed to be done, there would be no need to plan the darn restructuring.*

In fairness, the members of the inner circle probably didn't intend to stop conferring with their operating managers. And they might deny it if you leveled that accusation at them. They might admit that all those meetings with the consultants and the great urgency to reinvent have left precious little time for the friendly, personal interactions of more genteel days gone by. The single-minded focus on the restructuring that seizes the attention of top management, and the nonstop frenzy that accompanies it, are reminiscent of a condition that NASA employees call Go Fever. This term sprang out of the consuming pressure by top officials to launch manned rockets as scheduled—at just about any cost—during the days of the Apollo space program. This unrelenting concentration on the goal-at-all-costs spurred concern for astronaut safety. Today, a case of Go Fever can easily strike harried organizations rushing to implement Radical Change in the name of efficiency. The casualties may be employee livelihoods, product quality and, as pointed out above, even the organization's long-term viability.

DOCTORS MAY BURY THEIR MISTAKES; CONSULTANTS DON'T HAVE TO LIVE WITH THEIRS.

Dispirited and disenfranchised

Whatever the reason for top management's aloofness, most managers in the company soon realize that they are newly chartered members of the Outta-the-Loop Group. They're keenly aware that senior executives aren't seeking and don't seem to value their thinking on the challenges that face the organization. Refrains of frustration echo through the organization. Cynicism and resentment fester and grow. My friend Ron Taddei puts it this way, "When leaders get too far out in front of their troops, they stop leading the team and become the enemy." Not surprisingly, when the long-awaited Grand Plan is unveiled, the very managers who should be key to its success approach it with little enthusiasm, and a significant number may secretly hope it fails.

Summon your courage, swallow your pride and hold your tongue. You may feel shut out, but top management is counting on your help come implementation time. The game is hardly over when the consultants leave (though that may seem to be years away). When the Grand Plan fails to deliver as expected, you'll have ample opportunity—and accompanying receptivity—to present workable solutions from your real-world perspective. Meanwhile, endure, make notes and enjoy the show.

Short Take: Consultantspeak—Say what?

Management consultants tend to pepper their chart-laden reports, formal presentations and casual speech with metaphors ("Let's put that on middle management's radar screen") and abstract, multisyllabic words that, to be polite about it, one would call jargon. These strange phrases begin to creep into senior management's conversations, and before very long they regularly show up in official company memos, speeches and articles. My favorite illustration of this appears below. This parody is excerpted from a pseudo-employee newsletter circulated in a company embroiled in the midst of a major, consultant-led restructuring. I'd love to credit the writer of this inspired work, but (for obvious reasons) the piece appeared without identifying its author. The identity of the company and its consulting firm have been omitted.

The Management Committee recently set up six Cross-Functional Multipurpose Transition Implementation Task Support Teams that are responsible for facilitating the short- and medium-term interdepartmental process changes and multiple procedural workflow modifications expected under the newly transmogrified organizational architecture.

The [consulting] firm...will supervise and coordinate a systematic transitional contingency phase, providing appropriate terminological support, including requisite obfuscatory marginalia, wherever and whenever a potentiality for fiduciary or pecuniary remuneration obtrudes (not excepting the generation of commodious volumes of administrative disquisitions, thus facilitating multiple redundant invoice submissions).

[The consultants have] divided the reorganization into...distinct stages, or "chronosynclastic matrix-transformational morph-grids":

Grid A (Early Transition)
1. *Build new processes within each functional area.*
2. *Process new functions within each building area.*
3. *Function building within each new process area.*

Grid B (Mid-Transition)
1. *Resolve cross-functional issues.*
2. *Function across resolved issues.*
3. *Cross functionally resolved issues.*
4. *Issue cross-functional resolves.*

45

What the Consultants Planned

Everything

worked ▶ just   the   plan ▶ filled   jargon

perfectly ▶ in   high   with   and

priced   consult-ant's   fancy   symbol

What Actually Happened

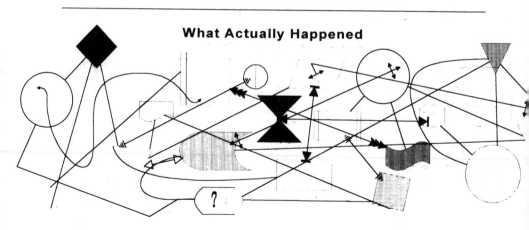

Grid C (Final Transition)

1. *Implement immediate preparation (of short-term changes).*
2. *Change short-term preparations (for immediate implementation).*
3. *Prepare for immediate termination (implement change of shorts).*

It is hoped that this rationalized, process-driven modality of trans-morphing the relational infrastructure will facilitate a broad, cross-hierarchical productivity empowerment. But if it doesn't, the company is prepared to assume major fiduciary encumbrances, liquidate superfluous physical-edifice assets or place hypertrophied wagers on equine competitive events, in order to be able to allocate sufficient fiduciary resources to accessing additional polysyllabic cool-sounding jargon. Whee!

The moving jigsaw puzzle

No plan works by saying "go." Plans that call for radical and massive change across an entire organization are bound to be incomplete and at least a little off-base no matter how much time and money were spent developing them. A whopping 68 percent of 350 executives involved with business reengineering interviewed by management consulting firm Arthur D. Little, Inc., said their reengineering projects "had unintended side effects and created new problems instead of solving old ones" (*InformationWeek*, June 20, 1994).

Knowing that the Grand Plan isn't going to work perfectly and is going to keep changing, you need to stay focused on why your organization underwent the Radical Change in the first place. You and your staff will have to make it up as you go along.

"Every day is a revelation" was a favorite expression of mine during my company's restructuring. An open mind and a resilient attitude will go a long way toward preserving your sanity and getting the work done.

Vacuum filling

SUMMON YOUR COURAGE, SWALLOW YOUR PRIDE AND HOLD YOUR TONGUE. THEN ROLL UP YOUR SLEEVES.

Because you're human, you'll face great temptation to condemn the Grand Plan's imperfections. Running hither and yon declaring, "This isn't working! This isn't working!" only wastes the time you need to accomplish the goals for which you're still held accountable. Sure, you resent the added stress. Sure, you'd like to rub senior managers' collective noses in their mess; even if you could, it wouldn't undo what's been done or do what you need done.

Later chapters of this book present a comprehensive model of management; in the immediate aftermath of a Radical Change, you'll need to function as an infantryman just given a field promotion. With inadequate warning, training or preparation, take command and move up the hill.

Here's an example of how to function as an infantryman. When my staff and I inherited—with virtually no notice—several functional areas in a downsizing that claimed 40 percent of the company's employees, I gave them two directives:

1. Find vacuums and fill them.
2. Using your good judgment, do whatever it takes to get the job done.

If you have hired competent people (see Chapter 9), a similar directive is all they need to hear in order to jump in and make things happen. I had, and mine did.

Chapter 3

The case against teamwork, empowerment and training

In this miniaturized microchip age of the "virtual office," it is easy to forget that the basics of running a business, even after Radical Change, remain fairly constant and essentially simple and have nothing to do with fashionable buzzwords.

Consider a little historical perspective: Despite even Radical Changes in (1) the world's economic and political landscape; (2) the goods and services businesses sell and (3) the technology used to create and sell them, the fundamental functions of and challenges to running a business change very little from year to year or decade to decade. Consider these ageless principles of business success:

- Tailor goods and services to meet customer needs and wants.
- Find the right people and keep them motivated.

REPEATING BUZZWORDS IN MEETINGS OR MEMOS DOESN'T EQUATE WITH CHANGING AN ORGANIZATION'S STRATEGIES OR TACTICS.

- Maintain an edge over competitors.
- Keep a close eye on expenses.
- Anticipate and react quickly to a changing world.

These were the principles our predecessors used a hundred years ago and the same ones our successors will apply in another hundred years, no matter how many Radical Changes thunder through the ages.

While the fundamentals at the core of managing an operation stay fairly constant, they seem to be highly volatile. When the whole world is swirling in a maelstrom of dramatic changes, even the rather stable fundamentals of business seem to be swept away, as well, in the violent currents of uncertainty. People who believe they are facing new problems look for new solutions, and so new buzzwords emerge to describe afresh the new variations on the old themes.

When you are weary and seeking relief from the stresses of managing the day's crises, the concepts described by the new buzzwords can seem seductive. They promise to—or at least stir hope that they will—deliver powerful antidotes to the ailments poisoning productivity and profitability. Seminars, articles, books and tapes relentlessly promote the latest management fashion: one-minute management, flat organizations, quality circles, vision statements, empowerment, learning organizations, the virtual organization, etc. With no shortage of new ideas, most managers continuously await the one idea that will magically master Radical Change.

Because you're a manager pressured to deliver sterling results from the carnage left by Radical Change, the latest "Panacea of the Month" can be mighty alluring. And that's why it's easy to find yourself repeating new buzzwords, advocating new "power concepts" and earnestly trying to change your organization to better fit the popular new mold. However, you might find that despite all their publicity, trendy management fashions may be neither desirable nor effective in meeting the unique needs, traditions and current mission of your post-Radical Change organization.

Repeating buzzwords in meetings or memos doesn't equate with changing an organization's strategies or tactics—though you'd be hard-pressed to convince some senior executives of that. So it's not unusual to find a firm's top management declaring a label as policy without anyone having understood the implications or developed a real program.

In the face of new terminology masquerading as the solution to all your problems, remember: There is no relationship between how often someone (even a very powerful someone) repeats a buzzword and when things actually change for the better.

Guess what? You're a team!

Teamwork has become one of those voguish management concepts that is oft repeated and never understood. As part of the Radical Change, you may receive a directive from on high that your organization will now end political fiefdoms, reject department isolation and use teamwork to do its work. Announcing it does not make it so.

Admittedly, teamwork is an appealing concept. A friend in the travel business likes to illustrate the ideal this way. He holds out a hand and says, "One grain of wheat is of no use to anybody." Then he cups both hands. "Many grains of wheat can make bread, which sustains man." Thrusting his cupped hands forward, he adds, "People are like these grains of wheat. Alone, we're nothing! Together, we can do great things!"

Teams certainly can elevate the power of one person toiling in isolation. Unfortunately, it's all too easy to misassign the team label to any random group of employees or to confuse the lack of antagonism between departments as teamwork. Asking people from disparate departments to show up at a meeting does not make them a team. True teams are composed of people who share common tasks, priorities and values. True teamwork implies commitment to a specific outcome on a deadline, achieved through equitable work distribution and cooperation with colleagues—who may at times disagree intensely but who respect and value each other's experience and perspective. True teams have a spirit, a collective fire that grows as it's fueled by progress toward a clear goal shared by all members of the team.

BEING A TEAM MEMBER IS A FOREIGN CONCEPT TO MANY EMPLOYEES AND MAY ACTUALLY BE ANTITHETICAL TO THEIR TRAINING AND EXPERIENCE.

Trying to achieve goals simply by pledging allegiance to the ideal of teamwork and forcing the organization to teem with teams—without the necessary skills and organizational support—is inadequate. The role of team member is likely a foreign concept to most and may actually be antithetical to your employees' training and experience. While the teamwork ethic encourages dispersing responsibility, monetary rewards for merit remain individual: contradictory messages about what the organization truly values.

When unprepared people find themselves thrust into a group which is a team in name only, how do they know who's responsible for the work? Who distributes the responsibilities and workload? Will that be done equitably? Will the team operate efficiently? Who makes that determination? What is the team's charter? What is its duration? Is the team held accountable for results? How? Who determines if it's successful? If the team does somehow succeed, who gets compensated for its accomplishments? Who assesses or rewards an individual's contribution to a team's output?

Collaboration: inefficient but productive?

In the wake of Radical Change, teams (in the form of committees and task forces) reproduce like rabbits. This effect has its roots in an admirable ethic: Involve as many people as possible in helping to shape the new organization. Unfortunately, again, good intentions aren't sufficient to produce good results; teamwork turns out to be a code word for countless, meandering meetings.

Team meetings composed of people not skilled in team dynamics become unguided, long-winded discussions with either heated arguments or overly drawn-out, overly polite exchanges designed to avoid even the appearance of disagreement between people who are not in synch. In this environment, influence gives way to impotence, as meetings drag on in the hope of wearing everyone down to a consensus.

These meetings provide endless opportunities for gossip, group therapy, pizza and deli sandwiches. Teamwork shouldn't necessarily be a socially fulfilling experience, and that's fine; great sports teams are great because they win, not because the players get along famously. Talking about work isn't the same as doing work. Moreover, many of the meetings after the Radical Change may center on trying to define the new policies and mores of the new Old Familiar, Inc. and have little or nothing to do with doing real work—the kind that serves customers and shareholders.

Another shortcoming of ill-defined teamwork is that many believe teamwork is equated with agreement. Some groups simply will never reach agreement on difficult, substantive issues. And that's why some teams seem never to produce anything— other than a schedule for additional meetings. It also accounts for why some teams produce the most mediocre results—the team members, trying very

Short Take: The Tyranny of Involvement

Old Familiar, Inc., emerging from the shock of Radical Change, may seek to increase employee participation in shaping the new organization—an admirable undertaking for sure. Curiously, the upshot may well be to subject employees to unprecedented levels of distraction in a phenomenon one might call The Tyranny of Involvement.

In this scheme, the benevolent employer showers its associates with surveys, memos, audio- or videotapes, newsletters, special reports and the like—all aimed at trying to support employees as they cope with the Radical Change. Additionally, employees are encouraged, perhaps invited, to participate in various task forces formed to evaluate and reshape policies on compensation, flex time, cost savings, and on and on. The impact can be like that of a boomerang that strikes in the back of the head.

All the admirable attempts to communicate result in a numbing wave of information overflow. Participating in task forces—no matter how important—eventually becomes a distracting, time-sucking obligation. The bottom line is that the laudable efforts deteriorate into counterproductive measures that detract from getting real work accomplished.

If you're in a position to either initiate or participate in such programs, am I suggesting that you not? No. But some worthwhile activities can take on lives of their own, growing out of proportion and canceling their intended benefits. As with all good things, seek moderation.

hard to be cooperative and collaborative, don't want to offend their colleagues, and so they compromise themselves and endorse the least objectionable recommendation. If truth in labeling were applied to many teams, they might be known as The Well-Intending Employee Committee for Inertia and Inaction.

A friend who works in administration at a unit of General Electric relates: "We spend so much time in team meetings, we have only two-and-a-half days a week to do the real work. Since the cutbacks in staff, we've all picked up more work, more useless meetings and much more stress!"

Poorly executed, the teamwork concept is extremely costly. Imagine calculating the return on investment for employee time spent in these meetings (multiplying the hourly wage of the participants by the actual time burned in the meetings) and then adding the cost of the lost opportunity to produce real work. It's little wonder that decisive, results-oriented managers become impatient with this kind of team process.

The methodology for producing work using a true team model is not self-evident. Plenty of good literature describes effective team management and details the intricacies of organizing and managing the team effort. I raise the issue here to alert you to the deep implications of assuming that teamwork is little more than assembling a group of co-workers and declaring them a team.

Empowerment (a.k.a. magic wand management)

Proponents of employee empowerment tout it as the moral opposite of managerial control. Its champions utter rallying cries of "Treat employees like adults," "Power to the people!" and "You own it!" Under the empowerment ideal, the directive to workers is, "Be useful, not obedient." The virtues attributed to empowered employees include autonomy, creativity and self-motivation.

Sounds idyllic. What's not to like? Well, for one thing, no one—executive and front-line employees alike—really seems to know what empowerment

Short Take: Sports teams are not analogous to work teams

- Sports teams play games with narrow and finely defined objectives within precisely prescribed rules of behavior, adjudicated by independent referees.
- Players on sports teams assume a specific and clear role.
- Sports teams know what game they're playing, how points are scored and how winners are determined after a limited time of competition.
- Performance of a sports team can be judged by easily measurable results.
- Sports teams compete openly in the public eye.
- Sports teams have specialized coaches teaching specific skills in the context of the overall team effort.
- Sports teams train before having to perform and don't defer their training to consultants.
- Sports teams have an off-season to relax, as well as intervals of rest between performances.
- Sports teams routinely trade and cut players who have no expectation of a life-long job or a role beyond the current season.

means. Do you? The dictionary definition speaks of investing one with official or legal authority. In Old Familiar, Inc., that might have happened by waving a magic wand and declaring, "Poof! You're empowered." Both manager and employee might like the idea of empowerment, but given the Radical Change, neither has a clear idea of how an individual contributor's formal authority has changed.

The reality of empowerment often means that managers are consumed by so many new tasks and responsibilities that they simply ignore front-line employees and no longer provide expertise and support. As such, empowerment equates to abandonment. The responsibility for results once assumed by a manager is now shifted to lower-level workers who do not draw managerial compensation. This shift in accountability is frightening to many employees who prefer to take direction and have someone else accountable; they fear the new empowerment concept is designed to provide "just enough rope to hang me." Just as empowerment can be off-putting and intimidating to the employees it's supposed to liberate, it can be threatening to managers who relish their role of responsibility-taker and results-deliverer.

Even when a well-meaning manager does release responsibility for day-to-day operating details, doing so can be awfully uncomfortable and lead to a dramatic relapse from "You're empowered!" to "You're insubordinate!" Consider the case of one executive I know. Following a Radical Change, this trusting, enthusiastic manager focused his attention on weightier issues than day-to-day operations. He bragged to his colleagues about not returning phone calls from his reports for at least four hours; that way, his staff would be forced to make decisions on their own. After some months of letting go of routine matters, he again began to express interest in the details of his operation. After poking around and discovering decisions not to his liking, he called his staff to a meeting. He berated them for exercising a "pocket veto" on plans he viewed favorably before he minimized his oversight of the nitty-gritty. I know this man didn't mislead his staff when giving them the impression that they had certain freedom and power. It's just that he thought he'd retained some agenda- and decision-making influence over his trusted reports.

I don't dispute the attractive qualities of the empowerment ideal, in which employees are responsible for their own performance, perhaps even for the design of their jobs' processes. I do denounce the buzzword's vagueness and, therefore, its danger to the manager or organization that claims to have infused employees with responsibility and entrepreneurial zeal while not specifying their limits or authority. Here's what I suggest: Replace the word empowerment with Individual Authority Management (I AM). In the I AM model, instead of saying to your people, "You're empowered," you say, "You are authorized to...and accountable for..."

When you begin to fill in the blanks, be as precise as you can. How many dollars can someone spend, discount or refund on their own personal authority? What approvals are necessary for certain procedures? You can't and shouldn't even try to anticipate every possibility. The more specific your guidelines for the most common decisions your people will need to make, the better and more consistent their judgments will be. To help guide people through the gray areas, clearly specify their mission. The better they understand what the organization is ultimately trying to accomplish, the better their decision-making about the issues facing their corner of the operation. Without clear objectives, people are empowered only to waste time.

No matter how well you define limits of control, to keep the operation moving along, people need

NO ONE REALLY SEEMS TO KNOW WHAT EMPOWERMENT MEANS.

61

latitude to make decisions. As a general guideline, I tell my staff to use their good judgment in the context of the company's mission to make decisions. I tell them that sometimes I will question their reasons for making a particular decision. My doing so doesn't mean they made the wrong one. It means I want to understand the thinking behind the decision. This is not a punitive or even corrective process. It is a learning process for both employee and manager. In asking about the decision process, as a manager, I may gain insight into the operation I wouldn't otherwise have. I may discover that the decision I would have made in the situation was not as appropriate as the employee's. If we disagree after the fact, my job is to explain why I might have made a different decision and then to discuss how similar issues might be handled in the future.

Employees may take more chances when they have more autonomy than when a boss is hovering over their shoulders. Some management pundits suggest that you tell your employees that it's okay to fail. Think seriously about that advice before issuing such a license to your employees. It's okay to fail? Everyone is human, everyone makes mistakes. It's not reasonable to expect perfection. But permission to fail? That's awfully broad leeway. I suggest you encourage experimentation within defined limits following a well-thought-out plan of action, and let people know that you tolerate little mistakes. But do not give blanket permission (and perhaps subtle encouragement) for failure.

Short Take: Butterfly to caterpillar?

Following a restructuring, senior management may regress from being apparently open, accessible and input-hungry to obviously insular, defensive and accusing.

The high-energy and cohesive transition team that had operated from a "war room," planning and executing the significant changes in the organization, degenerates into a tired, take-cover clique-under-siege that issues statements lamenting that the organization is responding neither fast enough nor well enough to the challenge of Radical Change.

The new motivational message running through the exhausted management's communiqués sounds like a twist on a familiar theme: *Take this job ...or shove it!*

Training

When Radical Change makes its dent on the organization, survival may depend on employees' ability to demonstrate new skills and ways of operating. To close the gap between the current and desired organizations, employees and their managers are often sent to training programs billed by their providers as having something just shy of miraculous powers: How to Do the Impossible in Three Easy Steps. Firms spend billions every year on consultants, books, videos, hotel rooms and other resources to provide employees with training. Is the money well spent? Does training equip people to deal with Radical Change?

The word training literally means "to drag"! In the corporate world, that may amount to truth in advertising: All too often, training has no credibility with the people who are supposed to benefit from it because they find training to be a drag. To get them to attend training programs, you need to drag them there. If most training programs really benefited their attendees, this wouldn't be the case. So what's wrong? Certainly the concept of developing new skills to help both the employee and the organization is a sound one. The failure is often in both the expectation and the execution.

Here's a basic truth at the root of the failure of training: Exposure to information doesn't cause a change in behavior. That's especially true when training is used to modify behavior rooted in belief. Does anyone seriously think that a training program to encourage diversity in hiring will mitigate a bigot's inclinations? Beliefs and long-remembered experiences exert much greater pull on us than new information, no matter how impressive its presentation. This is true even when looking at much more mundane training topics than attitudes. Shortly after being exposed to new information, people can't even recall it much less integrate it into making fundamental changes in their work lives. Addressing workplace challenges through training programs may amount to emergency treatment for a chronic condition.

Ron Taddei, who directs training for a national company and holds a master's degree in chemistry, asks, "What is the half-life of training?" (Half-life is the time required for radioactivity to be reduced to half its initial value.) The time required to cut in half the lasting impact of some training courses may not extend to the first coffee break.

EXPOSURE TO INFORMATION DOESN'T CAUSE A CHANGE IN BEHAVIOR.

There are other reasons many training programs don't deliver the expected thrust. Here are eight of the most common reasons:

1. People are forced to attend training. Someone with a basically dysfunctional personality may be sent to a "human relations" course. No training program will turn Adolf Hitler into Mother Teresa. And if training is viewed as punishment or a distasteful event to get past, it probably won't be wonderfully effective.

2. The trainees can't respect the trainer. Professional trainers, who often taught children in elementary or secondary schools prior to becoming trainers, often hold themselves out as competent to teach anything. They view their jobs as facilitating the learning process. Trainer-as-facilitator usually means someone who can push the "play" button on a videotape machine, who knows little or nothing firsthand about the challenges faced by the people in training and who resolves heated discussions or difficult questions by saying, "You have to go with what works for you."

3. Canned training programs, generic and rigid, often have marginal or no apparent relevance to attendees. Employees at a manufacturing company may have to sit through videos or role-play exercises designed for service company employees, or vice versa.

4. The training is inconsistent or in conflict with principles the organization really values.

The trainer brings a set of assumptions, methods and desired outcomes that may not be echoed by the institution paying the consulting fee. A common refrain chanted by employees at such courses is, "Why doesn't senior management take this course (or practice what they preach)!"

5. The training course stands in isolation with no post-training follow-up. Managers shuttle employees off to a course with a great-sounding title and expect the employee to come back to the job "fixed." If someone showed you how to hit a baseball just once, how good a hitter would you be? Similarly, a good student in training doesn't necessarily make for a good applier where it counts. There's a huge difference between being a star while role-playing in an artificially controlled environment and performing well in the face of chaotic circumstances on the job.

6. The training has no bearing in reality. What some trainers call exercises or simulations, others might call games or silliness. Developing team skills by frolicking in the woods is like holding a seance to develop communication skills. Entertaining, socially affirming outings may be a lot more fun than working, but how likely are they to permanently change behavior patterns back at the salt mines?

7. The training fails to account for people's different learning styles or the pace at which they learn. Not everyone absorbs new material by reading, listening or participating in a simulation. Some programs ignore this fact altogether. Others recognize it to a fault, repeating the content in so many ways that the repetition becomes torturously tedious, giving rise to class clowning and other kinds of nonproductive behaviors.

8. The training consists of too many over-simplifications, abstractions and distractions to deliver useful, lasting put-it-to-work value. When employees sit through training that fails to give them take-home value, they get nothing more than a forced, unproductive paid day away from their duties.

The fact that many training programs fail to deliver on their promises doesn't mean the organization shouldn't encourage employee learning. And it doesn't mean the organization should cancel all training programs. What it means for you as a manager is that you need to critically evaluate the training you or your staff would dedicate precious time to attending. It means closely monitoring the information your staff is exposed to in training so you can reinforce and apply it to practical situations. It means taking an active role in educating (literally, "to draw out insight" from) your employees. This responsibility is discussed in detail in Chapter 5.

Chapter 4

The evolving role of the post-restructuring manager

"It is almost as if you were frantically construct-ing another world while the world that you live in dissolves beneath your feet, and that your survival depends on completing this construction at least one second before the old habitation collapses."
— Tennessee Williams

Radical Change likely struck your organization like an earthquake, shaking up—perhaps tearing up—the traditional. The cataclysm wrenched away the comfortable, creating a void and rendering the traditional ways of managing work impotent. So there you stand amidst a shattered, twisted land-scape where the old, reliable bridges between tasks to do and getting them done have crumbled. How will you function? How will you clear a path to pro-ductivity through the rubble of the methods that once worked?

If your organization underwent its Radical Change by way of a true process reengineering, some of the routes from the old to the new will have

TURN "ACHIEVERS-IN-WAITING" INTO HIGHLY COMPETENT CONTRIBUTORS.

been mapped (with varying degrees of accuracy). But not all routes appear on even the very best process map because it fails to include navigation around human obstacles. In other words, you may now know that you need to move the work in an altered flow, but your chart can't show you how to get your staff to take the new route. That's a trail you have to blaze.

CEO of your department

How do you manage the critical human variable in a process-altering reengineering, a streamlining restructuring or a cost-chopping downsizing? The answer to this question lies in any mirror. Your actions as an individual boss matter more in affecting the performance of your staff than any other factor in the restructuring formula. After all, to your staff, who is "management"? You are. No matter how great the distance from your chair to the president's, you exert more day-to-day influence on the people reporting to you than anyone in the executive suite. This link was quantified by Wilson Learning Corp. when it surveyed more than 25,000 employees in a variety of companies. The employees reported that some 69 percent of their job satisfaction comes not from such factors as the hours they work or their financial incentives but from their boss's leadership skills.

As a boss, you've always had some impact on how your people perform, but now—in the face of tremendous upheaval, uncertainty and instability in the workplace—your influence on your staff is magnified. The Radical Change put your managerial muscles on steroids. The muscles you flex and how you flex them may well determine whether you and your staff get the better of the Radical Change or vice versa.

This effect was clearly demonstrated at my own workplace following the restructuring that trimmed the staff count by 40 percent. This dramatic change was accompanied by a new business model, one in which providing better service to both internal and external customers was a new imperative. Managers were explicitly expected to deal with their staff members in ways that encouraged them to be collaborative, take initiative and assume personal responsibility for the work they produced.

Several months into the Radical Change, it became apparent that effectiveness in the new organization was taking hold across it quite unevenly. Some pockets of the company eagerly embraced the new operating model, taking initiative, displaying creativity, reaching out to departments previously off-limits. Other corners of the company were demonstrably not so well adjusted—information was hoarded, cooperation with other units was much less enthusiastic and employees seemed terribly reluctant to take initiative or responsibility for changing from the old status quo. When we tried to account for these markedly different performances, an unmistakable pattern emerged: A department's ability to surmount the Radical Change was inextricably tied to the ethic embodied by its individual manager. Your call to duty as a manager, as a leader, is one of tremendous responsibility.

The new world

"The difficulty lies not in the new ideas but in escaping from the old ones," wrote British economist John Maynard Keynes. An old management idea, the military model of supervising work by top-down command and control, is both familiar and ego-gratifying to those in charge. But this management idea is inappropriate to managing in the environment created by Radical Change in which employees must be vested with more autonomy, more responsibility and, therefore, more trust and freedom.

"A new world is not made simply by trying to forget the old," wrote American author Henry Miller. "A new world is made with a new spirit, with new values." The new management model for making your corporate world work in the wake of Radical Change is predicated on a simple but difficult principle: As a manager, your job is to add value to the work of others while allowing them to shape and take responsibility for their own work.

I'll describe the particulars of this new model in detail following an important point. At the heart of adding value to the work of more autonomous workers—who are charged with generating more creative ideas, working with less supervision and support and assuming accountability previously relegated to management—is gaining their trust. This is the irony: Just when you need the best thinking and the hardest work from your shell-shocked survivors of Radical Change, they likely trust management the least. At the same time that employees have been asked to assume more work and responsibility, they're doing it for the same or reduced pay while their benefits may have been reduced or may cost them more.

This gives rise to a troubling paradox: Your organization cannot offer your employees security—and may actually promise the least job security of their careers, but you must create an environment in which people feel secure in their opportunity to succeed so that they'll work harder to do so.

Your job is to keep your staff on a steady course while they're being tossed about in Radical Change's waters of ambiguity. You need to do this amidst changing signals, mixed signals and no signals at all from top management. As you'll see later, one of the most potent acts you can perform is to proclaim your priorities for your people to keep them pointed toward the desired destination. Driving to a clearly defined destination, by whatever route, still requires thousands of minor adjustments along the way. In guiding those adjustments through the journey, you add value to mapping your way from the old to the new.

YOUR ROLE IS TO TAKE A GROUP OF COMPETENT PEOPLE AND LEAD THEM TO GREATNESS.

The Value-adding Manager

The rest of this book describes ways you can manage your way through the Revolution of Radical Change, channeling the energies of all to reap the

73

rich possibilities of your organization's new era. Central to these concepts is this assumption: With more demands on your time, higher expectations, fewer resources and more responsibilities, you simply cannot, in the classic sense, supervise the work of other people. The word "supervise" comes from the Latin *supervidêre*, "to see over," as in looking over someone's shoulder. In the days of bloated management ranks, managers could literally do that. Today, you cannot.

In the aftermath of Radical Change, your time cannot be spent double-checking; your role is not merely that of failure prevention. Your role as manager is to take a group of competent people and lead them to greatness. Your job is much more than riding herd on budgets, deadlines and performance to specifications. Your job is to add value to the work being done by talented, capable people.

The remaining chapters detail guiding principles and principal methods of the Value-adding Manager. Think of these recommendations as more of a recipe than a prescription, and understand that they are parts of a process, not ends unto themselves. Good management is like the wind: Only its effects are visible.

Part 2

Leadership skills for the new era

Chapter 5

Increasing competence and performance: Leader as educator

In the aftermath of the staff reductions forced by Radical Change, you'll be called upon to produce more and better work by expanding your staff's competence rather than its size. As you face this challenge, bear in mind that competence is much more than the particular skills one has mastered. What your staff members know how to do now will help them address your organization's problems from the past. What they can imagine, what they can create and the new knowledge they'll learn will enable them to help your organization create a successful future.

The mission of education in your new organization is not just about acquiring skills to solve specific problems but also expanding minds to address problems and opportunities that aren't apparent. In manual labor, repetition may be the mother of skill. In knowledge- and service-based work, interest in the work is the father of skill. Productivity in our high-tech, specialized-knowledge world is no longer simply about doing more work faster or at lower costs.

> YOUR JOB AS A LEADER IS NOT TO POSSESS OR CONTROL INFORMATION BUT TO ENCOURAGE YOUR PEOPLE TO ACQUIRE AND CREATE KNOWLEDGE.

Productivity in the knowledge and service economy is a function of imagination, ingenuity and constant improvement in the face of Radical Change. That productivity results from a constant upgrading of your organization's human resources. The continuing education of your staff cannot depend simply on sending people to an occasional program sponsored by your employer. Rather, continuing education is *your* constant obligation as a Value-adding Manager.

Worker as thinker

In today's service- and knowledge-based economy, just about every industry—and job—is driven by high technology and higher education. Since John Henry took on the steam shovel, workers have been required to acquire increasing skill to operate machinery that produces goods or performs even manual labor. They must use and constantly improve their knowledge and imagination. In disciplines outside those that produce tangible products, this truth is magnified, as employees' thinking often *is* the product.

The increasing intellectual sophistication necessary to earn a living has caused an evolution in the responsibility for thinking on the job. The old model of Boss as Idea Man has given way to a new paradigm in which knowledge and insight have no rank, and innovation as well as problem-solving is everyone's job. The evolution has taken hold with greater speed and elegance in some quarters than others. Old Model managers who see intellectual contribution as their exclusive domain and source of power are slow to surrender their grip. Recently, a friend who works in a publishing company (whose product is intellectual by its nature) told me about a planning meeting she attended in which some key players on a project were asked to leave by an Old Model boss because they didn't hold a "manager" title. The meeting dragged on unproductively because the participants needed information that the expelled attendees had gathered or were experts on.

In the new model, the Value-adding Manager isn't threatened by others' expertise, no matter where they sit on the organization chart. Your job as a leader is not to possess or control information but to encourage people to acquire and create knowledge that helps the organization become more effective. Some simple tactics make this charge an easy one to execute.

Rethinking job descriptions

One of your first tasks in fulfilling your role of leader-as-educator is to help employees to understand that their job descriptions are wholly inadequate in describing your expectations. Job descriptions, an outgrowth of the division of labor in large institutions, attempt to define what someone holding a given position should do. To fully describe a position implies that one knows most of what the job holder will confront in the position and what's expected to be done about it. In the Old Model organization, an outgrowth of a mostly predictable business and social environment, the job description was an instrument of clarity and efficiency. Radical Change, inside and outside your organization, altered that.

Now you must create a new tradition in which employees operate outside tradition. In the new, chaotic environment brought on by Radical Change, traditional job descriptions specifying duties limit, more than expand, the possibilities of employees taking initiative and filling vacuums. In addition, old-style job descriptions give no credit to the total package of skills, insights and experiences that an individual brings to the position. After all, every person you hire comes to the new position—no matter how precisely his or her resume matches the ideal candidate's background—with a unique set of experiences and insights. Each uniquely individual experience with another employer, a volunteer organization or any other establishment can add a new dimension to *any* position if you allow someone to contribute beyond fulfilling the prescribed tasks of the job description. When I think of my favorite teachers and bosses, they always had this trait in common: They always saw something in me, call it potential, that I did not see in myself. A Value-adding Manager sees the seed of greatness in everyone and works to nourish and cultivate it.

Contrast that approach with the customary job description that essentially says to employees, "Never mind what you know or can learn or the great things you might conceive of or do for Old Familiar, Inc. Your job is completely specified in great detail all right here on this piece of paper." Of course, today you cannot specify with any degree of accuracy exactly what someone's job will encompass because, ideally, it will change just about every day to stay competitive and in synch with the world. Job descriptions need to evolve from a grocery list of duties to a description of the job's likely outcomes and its potential scope of influence. An example:

"This position exists to help Acme Amalgamated produce quality widgets profitably. Generally, the person in this position will support that mission by working cooperatively with colleagues and taking responsibility for _____,
_____ and _____. At a minimum, the person in this job will utilize and keep up-to-date the skills necessary to continually improve the way in which the job's mission is accomplished..."

Just as it became habit to include in all job descriptions a phrase saying "other duties as assigned," you should add a new requirement to all your job descriptions:

"Your job requires that you contribute your best thinking to the organization; you are expected to share your unique experience, education and insight and to continue to add to your skills and education to help the organization meet the challenges it faces. You have an obligation to question and even challenge our policies and to suggest better ways of doing things."

Admittedly, this is a bit longer than "other duties as assigned," but it's a whole lot more relevant to

81

overcoming the organization's challenges. While it's fashionable to talk about creating a "learning organization," the most important thing you can do to make learning standard operating procedure is to make clear to your employees that you consider learning a fundamental part of every job—and a condition of employment.

Developing greatness

Revising the thrust of your staff's job descriptions is but the first of many steps you can take to become a catalyst for increasing competence among your achievers-in-waiting.

Clearly and specifically communicate the organization's short- and long-term objectives and your agenda for helping it achieve its goals. Having a clear sense of what's important and corresponding timetables helps people to make good, independent judgments when faced with competing priorities or a situation for which there is no policy or precedent.

Use your organization's useful training resources. While I was critical in Chapter 3 of the way some training is done, training is not inherently bad. Here are seven ways to make sure your staff is getting effective training:

1. Preview the information your staff will be exposed to. Ask the person responsible for the program for an outline of the course and some of its support material. Some off-the-shelf programs, such as those sold by Zenger-Miller, provide wallet-sized cards imprinted with key concepts supervisors can use to reinforce the information given to their staffs.

2. Volunteer to teach in your organization's employee education program. Don't worry about being a great instructor; you'll likely go through a certification course that will help you develop the instructional process part. If the certification course is any good, you'll learn about the dynamics of adult learning, differing learning styles and how to present course materials effectively.

Even if you've never formally taught before, you'll do fine. You bring to the table your passion for the business, your experiences (especially those that you painfully learned from) and your managerial insights. Line managers have credibility when they instruct fellow employees using professionally prepared course materials. Don't worry about being afraid to address a group. You do it every day. Besides, no one ever talks to a group; you can only communicate with one person at a time. It just so happens that speaking to a roomful is wonderfully efficient.

3. Provide daily learning opportunities. Your goal is to become a competence accelerator. Encourage people to take on projects and interact with colleagues they don't normally work with, in or outside of your own work group. Invite guest speakers to your staff meetings. Circulate magazine articles. Buy your staff books, tapes and newsletter subscriptions. Don't let cuts to the human resources or training budget or bureaucratic nonsense stand in the way of getting your people the resources they need to get better and better. If you have to, call the learning materials "office supplies." Isn't it amazing that companies routinely proclaim, "Employees are our most important asset," while spending far more on their upgrades to capital equipment than on their human capital? Don't let that myopia prevent you from continually upgrading the people responsible for continually performing to ever-higher standards. (One of my favorite examples of silly corporate policy involves an employee I had recently hired. She was long on brains but a bit short on practical experience related to her new duties. I asked her to attend a course at a local university to pick up some of the functional nitty-gritty she needed to know. Her request for funds from the HR education budget was rejected; seems that it only pays to educate employees who have been—wasting time?—on the payroll for at least a year!)

4. Question your employees constantly. In the fourth century B.C., Socrates showed us that the most effective method for teaching someone was not to tell them the answers but to ask them the questions. Insight, by definition, comes from within. You cannot force someone to understand a concept— that is, an internal process—and no two people understand anything exactly alike. To make the process of insight work for you and your staff, make a habit of asking nonthreatening questions to understand why your people do what they do the way they do. Chances are, your employees will learn as much as you do when you ask: Why did you do it this way?

What alternatives did you consider? If you could change the way we do things now to improve the process (to make it faster, cheaper or pleasing to more customers), how would you?

5. Require competence and test for it. True professionals must pass competency examinations to ply their trade. Why shouldn't that ethic extend to everyone holding themselves out as a competent purveyor of skills? Sure, some people will grouse that they shouldn't have to prove themselves after having done the job forever—which is especially why you should assess their current state. You can make the assessment exercise a positive experience by pointing out that you're doing it to maintain the highest standards and to assure the quality of your work group's output. Competent people have nothing to fear and may even have a chance to show how good they really are. After all, don't most competent people toil away in obscurity with their good work usually taken for granted?

6. Communicate that you expect employees to invest in themselves. In many organizations, this implies a significant change in the old implied contract in which the company historically assumed the burden of providing all skills improvement, usually along with managing an individual's career path. Now the obligation is shifted to, or at least shared by, employees.

Think of it this way: Your organization is buying a set of skills sold by an employee who represents that he or she is selling skilled and marketable labor.

THE MORE EACH INDIVIDUAL ON YOUR STAFF KNOWS, THE GREATER HIS OR HER POTENTIAL FOR MAKING A SIGNIFICANT CONTRIBUTION.

In the new economy, employers promise nothing more than to purchase the skills they need, and employees understand they have an obligation to sell marketable skills even though that increasingly means investing their own time and dollars to remain salable. Licensed professionals and tradespeople are often required to spend a minimum amount of time every year improving their skills. They may not like the obligation, but they know it's a way of staying current and assuring the people who retain their services that they are not relying on a 20-year-old body of knowledge. This requirement to stay current should apply even to long-tenured employees who may have begun to think of their place on the payroll (and all the benefits that come along with it) as an entitlement.

7. Give everyone the power of information. Old Model bosses were information brokers. They derived power from holding onto and brokering bits of information and knowledge. The less an Old Model boss's staff knew, the more power the boss had. Today, it's the exact opposite. The world changes so fast that no one can know all there is to know that would be powerfully useful, so trying to have an exclusive right to information is not just inefficient, it's foolhardy.

Instead of assuming an obligation to inform your staff on a need-to-know basis, change your approach to that of tell-me-what-I-need-to-know. In downsized organizations operating in our hurry-hurry-faster-faster economy, everyone knows something relevant and important that the boss may not. Not only should you not hoard the information you have, you have to make a point of tapping every source of information within your own little corner of the organization. But that's only the first step.

Equally important is sharing more and more information with your staff. The more each individual on your staff knows, the greater his or her potential for a significant contribution. In fact, by sharing everything but truly confidential information with your group, you may find your days shortening and your stress level lowering. The reason is simple: When your people have the information you do, they'll likely make the same, if not better, decisions than you would. This relieves you of the onerous obligation to consider all the information for every little decision. Be honest. For many routine decisions, aren't the capable people on your staff perfectly equipped to make a reasoned judgment?

One other benefit to providing your crew with the information they need to effectively navigate their way through the week: They will get increasingly better at making meaningful contributions to the enterprise. The more they know about the business, the more they can work to meet its goals.

Encourage "generative thinking." At the beginning of this chapter, I stated that problem-solving can only address the past. While encouraging your people to help solve the organization's problems certainly makes sense, it is less than half the formula for a successful future. Ask:

- What opportunities do we have to improve what we do?
- How might we change things so that our work goes more smoothly?
- What should we be thinking about for our future?
- What do our customers (internal or external) need that we're not providing them?
- In an ideal world, what changes could we make that would make a big difference to our customers?
- Now, given our less-than-ideal circumstances, how can we get close to that goal using our creativity?
- What experiences have you had with, or know about from, other companies that we might try to adapt here?

Seek internal insight before turning to consultants. An old saying has it that an expert is someone you don't know who comes from at least 50 miles out of town. This common attitude has been prevalent for eons and is even referred to in the New Testament. ("Jesus said unto them, A prophet is not without honor, save in his own country, and in his own house." — Matthew 13:57). In Chapter 2, I described a case in which senior management ignored the insights of its middle managers during a Radical

PEOPLE CAN'T GIVE YOU THE BEST OF THEIR THINKING IF THERE IS NO MECHANISM TO DO SO.

Change. Don't make the same mistake! When you're wrestling with a vexing challenge, don't go it alone and don't rush to bring in an outside consultant. Go first to those around you whose talents and insights you may have overlooked or inadequately challenged. And don't expect your people to rush to relieve your troubles just because they see you suffering. They're likely to wait, even if they have a solution at hand, until you ask for help. The act of your not asking will lead directly to the effect of their not helping.

Create and use a "New Ideas" channel. Let's say you say to your staff, "I need your ideas and really want to hear them." What reaction would you expect? Applause? Not likely. How about blank stares and looks of disbelief? More like it.

I attended a meeting at which a new corporate vice president had just gathered his new staff. With great humility and earnestness, he poured out his heart, saying how much he needed the participation of everyone in his new group. "I'm not smart enough to make it happen without your help. I need you to, and expect that you will, contribute your best thinking. Every idea is welcome. There's a place at the table for everyone. We're going to work together to make this the best place it can be. I'm depending on you." As the new executive was making his impassioned plea, I watched his audience. They fidgeted and darted or rolled their eyes. Afterward, I asked people for their reaction. "It was okay," people said with a sigh of disappointment. I retorted, "Gee, you seem kind of down; wasn't the speech inspiring?"

"Oh, he said all the right things, but I don't believe he meant them," came the reply.

People are simply not accustomed to a boss saying, "I need your ideas" and meaning it. Somewhere, sometime, long before you even met your staff, some boss said words to that effect to everyone who now reports to you. Perhaps they believed these words the first time they heard them—until they tried to pass along a precious idea that was rejected. Maybe they were ignored or insulted. In any case, they came to understand that "I need your ideas" was something bosses said but didn't mean.

Now let's assume that you have developed a trusting relationship with your staff. They know you're sincere when you ask for help. After they start to believe you really do want their suggestions, what do they do about it? Tackle you in the hall as you rush from meeting to meeting? Make an appointment to chat? Slip a note under your door? People can't give you the best of their thinking if there's no mechanism to do so.

One effective channel for making recommendations, raising important issues and suggesting new ways of running the business is an anonymous e-mail box. I implemented such a system at my workplace with great success. I had our technical guys rig our e-mail system to automatically strip the name of the sender from any message sent to an address we called NewIdeas. Messages sent to this address were routed to a small group of people who acted on the messages. We introduced the system with great fanfare during a time of Radical Change. We wanted people to know they had a direct line to senior management and could address important issues under the cover of anonymity. The program was so successful that the entire company adopted the concept, creating an interdisciplinary team to review and act on suggestions from employees in all departments at all levels.

When the topic of an anonymous feedback channel comes up, some people bristle, fearing either a load of nasty notes or the possibility that anonymity will encourage people to shirk responsibility for their suggestions. As for the nasty comments, sure, there are likely to be some. But the system in my company, while yielding thousands of well-thought-out and useful suggestions, received but a handful of sarcastic or meanspirited messages. I don't think this was because my company hired only angels. Rather, we did three things to secure the program's success:

1. Senior management communicated a sincere desire to get everyone's thinking during the turbulence of Radical Change, offering nothing more than their serious consideration to any respondent's message.

2. We made it clear that the system's anonymous feature was real and irrevocable. (Some correspondents had actually complained when they didn't receive a reply to their anonymous message!)

3. We reported on the suggestions and questions we received through this special channel. Some recommendations were immediately implemented; others were put into plans for action sometime later; still others were rejected with an explanation of why they wouldn't be implemented at this time.

For those who consider an anonymous system a device to veil responsibility for one's suggestions, here are some thoughts. First, anyone sending a message should have the option of including his or her name in the message and requesting a personal response. (In my experience, many people did this.) Second, and more significantly, the anonymous nature of the system encourages far, far, far more people than those who'd normally throw in their two cents' worth to participate. Some people do fear reprisals; others don't want attention for their contribution, just the positive change it might effect; others are simply shy and would otherwise cower at addressing the top brass but for the cover of anonymity. In any event, anonymity is a positive, not a negative, aspect of a well-intentioned and well-run system.

If your system is successful in attracting many suggestions, you'll have a wealth of new thinking to sort through. It's a nice problem to have, but it's a lot like hunting for pearls: The sorting takes a long time and requires wading through a fair amount of goo to find the rare gems. But the effort is worth it even if only one idea in a thousand holds the promise of improving your operation. The real impact comes in the morale boost that occurs when employees discover that management was serious when it proclaimed, "We want your ideas."

Provide higher learning for your senior people and star performers. You might be tempted to ignore the skill improvement needs of your top people—after all, they're doing great. But they may also be your best prospects for a high return on your education investment. They've demonstrated they can do well with the knowledge and skills they already have. Just imagine how much more skilled they might become when exposed to additional new insights.

Educate yourself. The more you know, the more you can help others. One of the keys to true improvement is to expand your repertoire, not just get marginally better at old competencies. Challenge yourself. Read a business book on a topic you don't normally read about (finance for computer people, market research for financiers, materials handling for marketers). Become a well-rounded individual who stays one step ahead, someone from whom your ever-improving staff can still learn.

KNOWLEDGE, INSIGHT AND COMPETENCE HAVE NO RANK.

Embody the company ideals. Quick, what are your current company themes (core values or mission statements)? Can you—and everyone on your staff—repeat them? If you and your group don't know the organization's guiding principles by heart, how can you take them to heart? If the slogans are empty, send one of those anonymous e-mail messages described earlier to the person responsible and explain why. If the slogans are to have any meaning,

93

you need to know them, repeat them and embody them.

Be a model role model. Sure it's trite to say, "Lead by example." But it's still the best advice. Emerson wrote that an organization is but the lengthened shadow of its leader. As the CEO of your department, you should cast a bright light and a long shadow. One of the nicest compliments I've received in my life came at an industry conference when I met one of my former employees. She had been recruited away for a much bigger job and salary than my organization could offer her. After some chitchat, she said something I will never forget. "When I took the new job, I was really excited but quickly over-whelmed," she said. "There were days I was sure I was in over my head. But when I felt lost, I'd sit back and ask myself, 'What would Don do in this situation?' and that's what I did!" I relay this story not for my own aggrandizement but to make the point that your staff is always watching, absorbing and evaluating. In the course of every day, give them something to remember.

Chapter 6

Creating and sustaining quality: Leader as quality assurer

If you've ever bought a product that broke shortly after you carefully unpacked it from its box (or the day after the warranty expired), or if you've ever been subjected to uncaring service (an oxymoron) from someone whose job is to help you, you probably can appreciate the nearly evangelistic movement for Total Quality Management (TQM) that continues to sweep through corporate corridors. TQM is a wonderful ideal that has attracted a tremendous amount of attention and generated an incalculable investment of time and effort by untold legions of managers. For all the time spent on the pursuit of near perfection, for all the systems used to measure results against nearly impossible standards, for all the fanfare surrounding quality-related competitions, TQM may have become a victim of its own popularity—devolving into one of those buzzwords I denounced in Chapter 3.

QUALITY IS AS MUCH PERSONAL ETHIC AS PROCESS AND MEASUREMENT.

The difficulty with TQM is the "T." Achieving total *anything* is difficult. To obtain "total quality" means to develop total control over an organization's processes and outputs—designing everything in fine detail and measuring every process and outcome with great precision. Physical processes and outcomes lend themselves to such quantification. But people—who are increasingly a vital component of the total product, if not the actual "product" your organization exists to provide—don't perform to four or six decimal points. Even the most mechanized system is people-dependent and thus not totally controllable. Yet people can—and must—produce quality work. And you're responsible for extracting it from them. To deliver consistent quality from your human capital, your quality effort must evolve from one that merely assesses the technical quality of your products into one in which your people operate in a quality way, encouraged by your managerial quality.

IQM: Individual Quality Management

Let's spend a moment on the human factor in the quality equation. In spite of all the process mapping, all the intricate systems redesigning and all the elaborate measurements of outcome, the quality produced by an organization (and the success or failure of any Radical Change) is still dependent on how individual employees approach their work. Delivering quality depends on every single person involved with the process. This simple truth is the reason you should think of your charge to deliver quality work and produce quality products as something far less ambitious than Total Quality Management. Frame it instead as Individual Quality Management (IQM).

In the IQM scheme, quality is as much personal ethic as process and measurement. Quality derives from an innate personal commitment to good work, which is perhaps observable but not necessarily measurable. This commitment should be inherent in anyone doing any job. While you can't always see a person's quality ethic, you often can hear it. When co-workers are gathered and discussing the means by which they make their daily bread, listen closely. What sounds like complaining is more likely frustration from people who are either inhibited or prohibited by their organization from producing quality.

Example: While on a business trip in Albany, New York, I encountered a delay that forced me to kill some time at the Amtrak train station. I went into the station's little coffee shop and ordered lunch. Seated at the counter were a few cab drivers who were also idling until the overdue train arrived. Like any group of workers, these fellows began grousing, and none too quietly. What struck me was the tenor of their grumbling; they weren't complaining about stingy tips, potholes or slow business. No, these road warriors were concerned that their cab company wasn't run as efficiently as it might be. The dispatcher got too far behind on handling calls from customers. The mechanic didn't fix the cars so that they worked. One driver asked another, "Okay, big shot, so what would you do if you ran the place?"

The other exclaimed, "If they put me in charge just for one day, I'd clean house—get rid of all the prima donnas!"

Understanding quality as a collection of behaviors by individual people means managing quality as a personal relationship as well as a series of individual commitments. An organization's "culture of quality" derives from a collective ethic in which everyone freely and fully assumes personal responsibility for results. Such a culture is not a program, slogan or even a system of measurement. Rather, it is a value shared by all individuals.

To encourage this culture, create an atmosphere in which you trust your employees to act responsibly, work hard and do the right thing—even when everyone is straining to cope with Radical Change. You must not only trust those who report to you but also be trustworthy yourself, providing your staff with a suitable environment, tools, education and forgiveness so they can do a quality job. By forgiveness, I mean acceptance of the undeniable reality that human beings make mistakes—no matter how diligent, conscientious and careful they are and regardless of the organization's standards, measures and consequences for doing quality work. When employees know they work in a place that expects near perfection but forgives something less than that, they are much more inclined to come forward and admit—and more importantly, to point out—work that falls short of the desired mark. When workers at all levels are secure about coming forward, the

QUALITY DERIVES FROM A PERSONAL COMMITMENT TO GOOD WORK, WHICH IS OBSERVABLE BUT NOT MEASURABLE.

organization has a much better chance of delivering consistently high quality than when employees fear reprisal for substandard work. Such fears lead not to improved quality but to more and more elaborate schemes to hide errors and fudge the detailed reports that elaborate TQM efforts inevitably require. All the while they pretend that they're getting quality to spec—without fooling customers about what's really being delivered.

An example. I ordered a new Jeep Wrangler—a real Jeep, the kind that rides like an off-road experience even while driving across a sheet of glass. I had wanted this vehicle for some time and waited with great expectation during the nine weeks it took to build my custom-designed fantasy. Finally, the salesman called with the words I had anticipated for more than a decade, "Don, come in and pick up your new Jeep!"

I rushed down to the showroom, looking over that magnificent, shiny piece of Americana. My new pleasure craft had my custom-ordered pearl finish paint job. It had the leather-wrapped steering wheel, which matched the sand-colored interior, which matched the sand-colored removable top, and so on. A dream come true.

Right before I signed the final paperwork and handed over the final check, Dave, the friendly salesman, urged me to get in the front seat and feel that leather-wrapped steering wheel. It was a sensual delight, and I wanted to run back into the showroom to sign whatever paper was necessary to get the keys. As I started to exit from the Jeep's perch, I put my hand on the center console and detected a little wiggle. "Gee, Dave," I said with great reluctance, "this seems a little loose."

"No problem!" Dave said. "Let's finish the paperwork, and I'll tighten up the bolts with my own tool kit so you won't have to wait for a service bay." *Wow!* I thought. *Dave is an IQM/ethic-of-quality guy.* We signed the papers. Dave got his tool kit and tightened the bolts, and I drove off the lot and over to the Wendy's restaurant right next door. After finishing my chicken sandwich, I grabbed a handful of napkins—can't have too many of those in a new vehicle. I opened the lid to the center console to stash the napkins, and the entire console lifted right off the floor! I could see the pavement right through the many misdrilled holes—and there were no nuts to hold the bolts now dangling in midair from the bottom of the console. I returned to the dealership, where I proceeded to wait two hours for a service bay.

So what's the point? Someone had a bad day at the Jeep factory? No. This little tale goes much deeper than that. It represents the worst of TQM and the utter failure of IQM—even though I'm focusing on but one of the many thousands of parts that went into the building of my Jeep.

How is it the worst of TQM? When I returned to the dealership, I was shown two reports that said that the vehicle had passed quality inspections at both the factory and at the dealership. One of the items checked off on the forms warranted that all parts and fixtures were tightly fastened. As part of a quality program, executives at the dealership and at Chrysler, which makes Jeeps, were going to get a report, sworn to by individuals at the factory and the dealership, that I had received a vehicle meeting their quality standards. Dave, the apparently quality kind of guy, told me about a satisfaction survey I'd be receiving in the mail. "Incomes are tied to the results of that survey," he said with an almost pleading tone. "Would appreciate your checking the boxes down the right side of the paper," he said, referring to the "very satisfied" category. If I had done that (I did not), I would have been a coconspirator in the TQM lie that would show quantifiably that I had received a vehicle that met high-quality standards when it did not.

Granted, a loose center console is not a loose axle. But look at how this little item represents a breakdown in the IQM ethic. Those misdrilled holes were not an oversight. The individual who made the first of a whole chain of mess-ups certainly knew that the job wasn't done correctly. So did the person who tried but couldn't tighten the nuts on the bolts that spun around and around in misdrilled holes. So did the inspector(s) at the factory who signed a form saying all fittings were tight. So did the inspector at the dealership. So did Dave, who pretended to deliver quality, when he took his ratchet wrench and gave those hapless dangling bolts a few more wild spins in midair.

All of these people pretended to partake in a quality effort. And all failed to live up to the ethic of taking personal responsibility for delivering quality results. Not one of these conspirators stepped up to the challenge to say, "Hey, wait a minute. We're building this Jeep for Don. Let's give him the quality product he's expecting. Let's not try to pass this shoddy effort off as the quality we should deliver to our customer."

I blame each of the individuals in this sad chain. And I blame their managers for not creating a culture of quality in which people are comfortable—and encouraged—to come forward to report substandard work without fear of reprisal. Instead, everyone went through the motions of delivering quality and delivered disappointment in its place.

The console's coming apart (one of several minor annoyances) was the least of my concerns. What really spooked me was my fear that the same lack of honesty in quality might manifest itself in places not so evident, such as the engine block or the braking system.

Understanding a culture of work

Quality results when everyone in the organization expects to do excellent work and then performs in a manner that delivers quality. Several factors combine to determine work quality. Individual attitudes, the corporate culture (unwritten but institutionalized values) and the physical support systems the organization provides to employees all influence its quality of work. And all of these factors are *far* more influential to an employee's actual output than management's official edicts endorsing quality. (Refer to the Work Motivation Pyramid on page 103.)

WHEN HELD TO HIGH EXPECTATIONS AND SUPPORTED BY MANAGEMENT, WORKERS STRIVE TO DELIVER THEIR BEST.

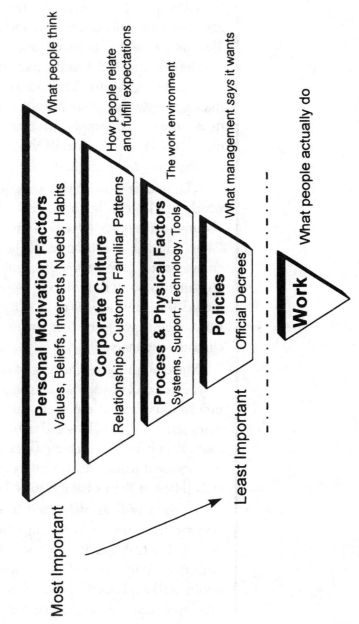

The Work Motivation Pyramid

Official organizational policies influence actual work output
<u>less</u> than any other factor.

Personal Motivation Factors
Values, Beliefs, Interests, Needs, Habits

What people think

Corporate Culture
Relationships, Customs, Familiar Patterns

How people relate
and fulfill expectations

Process & Physical Factors
Systems, Support, Technology, Tools

The work environment

Policies
Official Decrees

What management says it wants

Work

What people actually do

Most Important

Least Important

Let's apply this concept to the real world. Management may announce, "We must have quality!" This proclamation translates into expectations that are defined and fulfilled by internal measurements and reams of forms. That same quality-insistent management may not support its mandate with adequate resources or support to achieve the prescribed end result. It may also saddle the organization while cutting costs and cycle time.

The people who do the work quickly figure out which of the conflicting orders—true quality vs. documented quality—really counts with the brass. Guess which goal gets accomplished? This is how a company can have reams of quantifiable data that absolutely prove it is producing high quality goods in record time and at low cost, while still producing substandard products that anger employees and alienate customers.

Make no mistake: There is no contest in an employee's mind between what management's memos proclaim as desired outcomes and the results that management truly values and only subtly communicates. People resolve such conflicts quickly by giving management what it really wants even if that is radically different than what it claims it wants.

Workers who innately want to do quality work become frustrated by not being given the tools and time to do a truly quality job. Their attitude becomes defeatist: "Why bother?" They lose faith in their double-talking bosses. Feeling cheated and stressed, employees don't bother to go the extra mile required to deliver a quality product. In fact, they may do an increasingly poorer job—all the while completing reports to the contrary—as a way of punishing their superiors for trapping them in quality goals that are professed but impossible to reach with the current level of support.

Happily, the converse is equally true. Management that values true quality rewards a job well done regardless of how specifically its expectations are documented in some manual somewhere. When held to high expectations and supported by management, workers strive to deliver their best. They work harder to achieve top results even when that's not easy. Individuals who strive for greatness can perform against the odds when they believe management truly wants them to create quality output and backs up its commitment with an honest, even if not an ideal, level of support.

The lesson? While it's arguably an excellent practice to standardize process and methods and to quantify your group's progress against quality goals, understand that quantifying quality standards does not assure them. To achieve true quality, the measures must have meaning. When you, as a Value-adding Manager, provide your employees with the encouragement and dedicated support that embody the ethic of quality, measures serve as motivators to quality, not just report cards on them. Your people will then view mediocrity, not management, as the enemy.

Managing for IQM

Good management is ethic-, relationship- and process-based. While the ethic of managing for quality is essential to delivering quality, simply having an IQM moral code at work is not enough to deliver stellar results from your operation. To change work, you must change the culture surrounding it. Let's look at seven important principles that you as a Value-adding Manager can put to work so your group delivers quality.

Principle #1: Identify functions of value vs. housekeeping.

One reason workers sometimes get caught in the impossible bind between trying to meet unreasonable expectations and delivering quality is because they're forced to spend much of their time on dumb activities that do little or nothing to produce a quality product at a competitive and profitable price. The conflict here is between Assigned Activity and Expected Performance. When people spend time on things that don't matter, it takes away from their ability to produce things that do.

Example: I attended a seminar that featured a sharp market analyst for one of the world's largest brokerage houses. He detailed the daunting challenge of fulfilling his employer's requirement for a fresh list of prospects that included 10 million names a year. He performed a thorough review of the relationship between massive prospecting and subsequent, long-term sales success. His analysis showed a most disappointing correlation. Even after clearly demonstrating that targeting a much smaller number of higher quality prospects leads to much larger sales and profits, the requirement for the 10 million names remained. Senior management persisted in insisting that the firm's many brokers continue playing dialing for dollars on a massive scale so they would have something to do all day—a classic case of activity triumphing over performance.

The three functions of value

The necessity to trim tasks in response to tighter budgets and smaller staffs (a common outcome of Radical Change) is the perfect reason to evaluate your area's work. Most likely, incalculable hours and dollars are frittered away on work that makes no contribution to your organization or its customers. Your job is to identify activities that make a difference— that add value—and eliminate those that don't. Activities that add value typically have three outcomes:

1. Increased revenues.
2. Reduced costs without harm to quality (as defined by customers).
3. Improved products or services that entice customers to buy more from your organization and prefer buying from your organization rather than from a competitor.

If you or your people are spending time on anything that doesn't produce one of those three

IN SETTING PRIORITIES, GIVE UP DOING SOME THINGS ALTOGETHER TO DO OTHERS WELL.

outcomes, you're wasting precious time and corporate resources. And to those who would engineer an organization's Radical Change, such activities are therefore expendable.

The 3Rs of inefficiency

Even if you look at the work you're responsible for and can honestly say that all of it legitimately adds value to the organization, how efficiently does it do so? Your task now is to eliminate the 3Rs of inefficiency that drag on productivity and get in the way of producing quality work. The 3Rs of inefficiency are:

- Routine.
- Redundancy.
- Ridiculousness.

Saying that something is routine may be shorthand for "we've always done it that way." Maybe you have, but that doesn't mean it's necessary or central to meeting the organization's goals. After enduring a Radical Change, be clear with your staff about priorities. With more demands and fewer resources, not every task completed before will be completed now. Be honest with yourself and your staff about that. Maybe your group used to do a hundred different routine things a month, but now there's only time to reasonably accomplish 65 tasks. Don't force your people to guess which are the ones you really want done. Everything may seem important, but recognize that you can't expect everything to be done as before simply because it's routine.

The DIM-5 Principle

A scheme for evaluating your work is what I call the DIM-5 Principle. DIM-5 stands for Does It Matter in 5 Years, Months, Weeks, Days or Minutes? The point is to think about the longevity of the work you're facing when trying to decide between competing priorities. It's easy to get caught up in the urgent at the expense of the important. Some seemingly urgent matters just aren't important when viewed in terms of their relative impact on the organization over time. Your priorities, the work you choose to emphasize to the exclusion of other work, must reflect this time value to serve the organization's best interests.

In setting priorities, give up doing some things altogether to do others well. Otherwise, you end up with poor work on everything. Then, when all your customers have left you, what will it matter that you can report that you completed all the routine work?

Perhaps unearthing redundant work will be an easier task. Your group may be duplicating work within your own unit or replicating tasks that are also being done elsewhere in the organization. The easiest way to find out is to ask your staffers. They'll probably know, welcome your interest in eliminating make-work and help you identify other, more productive uses of their time.

As for ridiculousness, maybe there isn't much of that left after sustaining the rigors of the Radical Change. But before you're so sure, think about ridiculous work in this context: Perhaps you're performing tasks that your organization believes provides extraordinary service or benefits to your customers (unusual hours, exceptional customization, generous return policies, etc.). Are you sure they value it in proportion to what it costs to provide? Don't guess or rely on customer preferences from some years back that may have changed. Find out for sure and eliminate work that doesn't pull its weight, even though it appears to fall into one of the three high-value categories.

HONESTLY ASSESS YOUR CURRENT STATE WHEN DEFINING YOUR IDEAL STATE.

Question your work

To evaluate the tasks you perform, sit down with your staff and honestly find answers to these simple questions:

- Must we do what we're doing?
- If so, can we do it differently (faster, cheaper or less frequently)?
- What are the real consequences of our *not* doing it?

If you decide to stop doing an activity, set and announce a date for the change. Then stop doing it.

**The amount of work
you and your staff
have to do.**

**The amount of work
you and your staff
can do.**

**Set clear priorities for _high-value_ work.
Do that selected work well.
The rest simply won't get done.
Trying to do *everything* leads, at best, to mediocrity;
at worst, to total breakdown and disaster.**

Playing business

Your personal, managerial activities also must undergo rigorous scrutiny when evaluating your group's work. Much of a day or a week for managers and the people they supervise can be consumed by what I call "playing business." Playing business occurs when otherwise smart people go through unproductive motions that make no contribution to the enterprise. Like participating in unfocused meetings or spending time to review and give rubber stamp approval to paperwork that other, fully competent people have reviewed and approved when no matters of consequence or significant dollars are even at stake. Or allowing a meeting with a colleague to spin out onto unrelated topics (like the vagaries of lawn or car care or the latest movies). And on and on goes the list of time evaporators that may look like meaningful work but are not—not by any wild stretch of the imagination.

Principle #2: Specify (realistically) high standards and the processes to achieve them.

Quality is not absolute but relative. Customers, competitors and economics all shape quality. Above all, customers—not senior management's intuition or a consulting firm's "best practices benchmarks"— should drive the definition of quality. Benchmarks may be off the mark for your organization's objectives. The state-of-the-art is something of which you should be aware but not to which you should auto-matically aspire to replicate or improve upon. Delivering quality doesn't always mean providing the best or most extensive features or durability. Consider relative value to balance your target customer needs and expectations, the capacity of your organization to deliver on its goals and the value your customers believe they receive for their money.

Setting standards is a judgment call that requires you to balance resources, customer preferences, competitive dynamics and other factors. In health care, for example, regulatory and economic concerns are forcing some agonizing reevaluations of what constitutes quality. Delivering quality health care today (as defined by government agencies or insurance companies) may mean providing a level of service well below what might be technologically possible.

The current capabilities of your organization significantly color how well and how fast you deliver what you've defined as quality. If you lack qualified personnel (technical or managerial), adequate financing or sufficient infrastructure to support your ambitions, you won't be able to deliver on those ambitions. Honestly assess your current state when defining your ideal state. Plan to bridge that gap in a realistic time frame. Otherwise, you're setting up the organization for a demoralizing and fiscally damaging failure.

Dead people don't do quality

In assessing the standards to require your staff to meet, don't push your people too far. Simply trimming the staff and telling them to work "harder and smarter" may get the full workload done—for a very short time. Fatigue, stress and burnout will soon take their toll. An appropriate metaphor drawn from the pharmaceutical industry should serve as a graphic reminder. Drugs are tested on animals to determine the dose of the drug that kills 50 percent of the test group. That lethal dosage is known as the drug's LD-50. You must reevaluate your performance expectations long before you reach the LD-50 for your employees. People on the brink of exhaustion or burnout aren't going to deliver quality work consistently, if they deliver it at all.

Keep process prescriptions in perspective

Consistency in execution is the heart of quality. Humanity remains its soul. There is a natural tension between tightly specifying how work is to be done and considering the individuality of the people you employ to do it. The way to get better, faster and more efficient is to experiment, to challenge the tried and true and to allow the people who do the work to have a loud say in its design and an integral part in maintaining its quality.

Process drives quality, especially when caring, creative contributors drive the process.

Principle #3: Communicate goals.

Be clear in your own mind—and just as clear to your staff through your own words and actions—

about what you mean when you say you want quality. If you can't define acceptable outcomes, you probably won't get them or won't recognize them when you do. Your employees have a right to know what standard they're trying to reach and uphold.

As mentioned earlier, the definition of quality in your organization can change. Expect some employees to resist such change. The TQM movement that swept through corporate America a few years back did so with an almost religious fervor, complete with an ideology that was ascribed to quality as almost sacred. In addition, some elaborate internal mechanisms (to collect, codify and disseminate an endless stream of data) may have evolved in your organization to support the quality transformation. Some of your employees may have come to assume that this structure is necessary to produce quality. Employees may also have come to associate certain processes, work habits or employment benefits with producing quality work (for example, the paltry number of hours flight attendants were once limited to fly in a month).

Along comes Radical Change, redefining the infrastructure the organization can afford to support quality—a change that can have an impact similar to that of forcing people to convert to another religion. Naturally, you're going to encounter resistance. Expect it, and deal with it forthrightly. The world has changed, and we must change with it, even if it isn't how we would have designed the system.

WHAT IS REWARDING GETS DONE.

115

Communicate for tomorrow

When communicating about quality goals, give employees as much of a context as possible: what your customers expect, where your organization stands competitively and where you're heading strategically. Today's quality initiatives should support tomorrow's vision. That is to say, whatever your organization is today is but the forerunner of what it should be planning to become in the near future. That may be a slight or a great departure from the status quo, but your quality standards should be evolving to support tomorrow's requirements as well as today's.

Remember communication is (at least) two-way

Communicating quality standards is not merely issuing specifications and process plans. Communicating quality standards consists of a dialogue between everyone involved in a given piece of a process: workers, management and suppliers. Beyond that, assess the satisfaction of your work force with their contribution to the quality process. By this, I don't mean determining if everyone whistles while they work. Employee satisfaction in this context means determining (probably by formal and anonymous surveys) whether your staff feel they understand what management is trying to achieve and whether they feel they have the necessary tools, time, systems and management support to achieve their objectives.

You cannot dictate quality. You can specify desired outcomes, but you must communicate to achieve them.

Principle #4: Provide skill education.

When defining quality and the outcomes you expect your people to produce with finite resources, assess how well-equipped they are to meet the new expectations. Employees' skills and expected outcomes must align or you'll miss the target. In thinking about this simple truth, I'm reminded of two concert performances by high school musicians. The first concert featured a jazz group preparing for an awards competition. As the young artists executed their technically demanding repertoire, they were clearly struggling through it. Their leader, a teacher who obviously cared deeply about the music, began conducting with great energy. He waved his baton in a frenzy. He began jumping up and down and gesturing wildly. The more intense he became, the more astray they seemed to go. Finally, at the completion of the last note, the weary maestro turned to the politely applauding audience, a look of disappointment unmistakable on his face. Despite his intense, even heroic efforts, he could not single-handedly pull music from those kids that they just weren't ready to produce.

I thought of this man's futile effort recently while attending another concert, this one by choral students directed by a conductor with quite a different approach. As these young people flawlessly uttered convoluted Latin phrases in a complex, discordant and syncopated harmony, they were confident, relaxed, "in the groove" as musicians say. Before every number, each one more intricate and demanding than the one before it, their conductor smiled ever so slightly that smile of quiet confidence that communicated to his youthful charges: "I trust you; I know you're going to do a great job. And I'm right here with you to help." During the technically challenging passages, he reveled in those kids' success. They were one, as a single unit, enjoying the difficulty and rejoicing in mastering the moment. The singers and their leader had a special bond of mutual trust and admiration. As the students navigated their way through difficult passages, this bond fueled their energy rather than depleting it. They sang for their leader, who clearly had set some very high quality standards, and their hard work was repaid with respect.

Both of these dedicated conductors had high expectations for their charges. One delivered, one didn't. While I know nothing of the specific circumstances in either case, I'd bet that both were working with bright, talented and capable students but one invested more of himself in preparing his students for the challenges he was going to ask them to meet. And so it is with your own crew. Without preparation, you can't achieve goals that require your staff to perform to a new standard. Even your undying confidence, faith and respect get you only so far; preparation takes you the rest of the way. Help your staff develop the technical competence they'll need.

Prepare your people to meet the challenges you'd like them to sing their way through.

Principle #5: Insist on meeting goals.

Quality is not effort but achievement. If you have the right people on your staff (see Chapter 9), they'll appreciate your setting high standards to attain and maintain. Challenge is motivating!

Earlier, I mentioned the power of forgiveness in encouraging great work. While it is inevitable that your competent staff make mistakes, insist that they make any given mistake only once. After a mistake has been made, institutionalize a systemic fix to prevent the error from being repeated. Quality is not perfection but a system running to expectation. When that expectation is not met, the system needs correcting so that it can be met in the future.

Mistakes lead to greatness

Recognize that every mistake presents not only an opportunity to learn but perhaps the key to a new success. I once attended a seminar by world-renowned adventure photographer Galen Rowell. To be helpful to the enthusiasts who had traveled to hear this master's pearls of wisdom, he showed us a series of terrible slides from early in his development as a professional photographer. There were dark, underexposed pictures; washed-out, over-exposed slides; blurred and unfocused shots of scenery. "These are all common mistakes," he assured us. In

119

a delightful twist, he went on to point out, "The cause of every failure can be the cause of a great success." Then Rowell showed us stunning photographs he'd taken in which he had intentionally under- or overexposed the picture or used a blurred or unusual focus to great effect.

Like every great craftsman, Galen Rowell learned from his mistakes and used those lessons to great advantage. The annals of science, business and every other aspect of human endeavor are filled with fascinating anecdotes of how alert and creative individuals turned "mistakes" into opportunities to improve the world with new inventions (including chocolate chip cookies), insights and processes.

In assessing whether you've achieved the standard you were striving to meet, you'll likely want some objective measure by which you (regularly) rate your performance against the goal. I have no argument with that but hasten to point out that measurement has no value unless it is used to affect behavior or processes that have a greater worth than the cost of the measurement effort.

Principle #6: Reward for achieving quality.

When you hit your goals, celebrate! In the process, make sure your staff doesn't confuse the completion of any task with accomplishment. One way to make the difference clear is by only tying rewards for everyone involved to *meaningful* success.

Consequences influence behavior, as do no consequences. More on this in the next chapter.

Principle #7: Check with customers and revise the standards.

In your quest for relevant quality, routinely assess customer satisfaction with what you've delivered, as well as with your customers' expectations for the future. Adjust, not necessarily raise, standards. Make sure you know what attributes your customers value as constituting quality, and then consistently provide as much of that value as you possibly can.

Total quality, a worthy and difficult objective, is not and cannot be an end unto itself. Quality is the natural outgrowth when everyone in your organization works with an ethic of responsibility for quality results.

Chapter 7

Encouraging and rewarding high performance: Leader as cheerleader

In one of the men's bathrooms at the Hyatt Hotel in downtown Columbus, Ohio, right across the street from the headquarters of the Nationwide Insurance Co., a sticker someone placed upon a hand dryer contains the following message: "To hear the company president's annual message to employees, please press button."

Wouldn't you love to have a dollar for every time someone in management wrote in a self-serving PR piece or stood before a group of employees and said, "Here at Old Familiar, Inc., our people are our most important asset"? This trite bit of corporate-speak has been so oft repeated that it seems there must be a law requiring managers to repeat this phrase at least a few times a year or face severe fines and imprisonment. Now let's view that idea from a different perspective. Suppose contests were held

THE MORE INTENSELY MANAGEMENT TRIES TO PUSH THE NEW, THE MORE RESOLUTELY EMPLOYEES WILL CLING TO THE OLD.

in which you were awarded for treating your employees as though they actually were the most important asset of your organization. Would you win the prize?

Say tah-tah to rah-rah

Despite the lip service given to most organizations' alleged appreciation for the value of their human capital, you'd be hard-pressed to gather much proof that most people on the payroll are treated as the firm's most valuable asset. An entire industry has grown around the business of instructing managers to provide "motivation" to otherwise underappreciated employees. Gurus of this elusive art (most of whom never have managed in anything but a consulting firm) have become millionaires purveying seminars, books, audio- and videotapes that purport to help bosses turn workers who feel used and abused into people who want to work even harder and longer hours.

I use the word "cheerleader" as something of a caricature for an important role of a Value-adding Manager. This role is one of encouraging and recognizing top performance. I am not suggesting you bring pompons to your shop. Even when times are good, there's ample reason to be cynical about rah-rah in the workplace. Empty, feel-good boosterism seems especially out of character when picking up the pieces from a blast of Radical Change. There is something dishonest and offensive about trying to whip up enthusiasm in a situation in which former colleagues were dismissed and the increased workload exceeds resources and support. Under conditions like these, the job of a Value-adding Manager is not to preach the joys of thriving on chaos. Rather, it is to reduce distraction, restore calm, recreate confidence in otherwise rattled and frazzled employees and do the hard work necessary to encourage employees to buy into the organization's change.

Cultural Drag

As your employees confront Radical Change, expect them—even otherwise good-natured hard workers—to resist the mandated new ways. The more intensely management tries to push the New, the more resolutely employees will cling to the Old. A furious attempt to radically alter the way an organization does business will run smack into Cultural Drag, in which employees who've grown comfortable with the style, benefits and rituals of "the way things work around here" refuse to surrender familiar habits. They passively oppose management's attempts to kill the old ways to give birth to new ones.

The cliché "People resist change" is true only to the extent that people resist any change they believe offers less payoff or more pain than what they've come to know and love (or at least tolerate). Losing Old Familiar, Inc., need not be a traumatic experience.

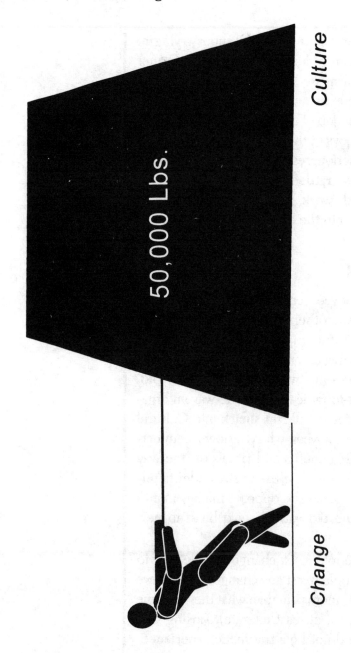

50,000 Lbs.

Culture

Change

An established organizational culture can be a real drag on a forward change movement.

You can address your employees' inclination to resist change by going to the trouble of identifying and pointing out whatever positives lurk in the dark corners of the Radical Change. Some of the benefits of the unsettling changes might not be realized for many months; acknowledge that fact. Communicate that you understand that today's immediate pain seems a high price to pay for a future benefit to your organization.

Try to present a perspective in which the payoff in building a stronger, more competitive organization is worth the price of the upheaval. As much as you reasonably can, make meeting the challenge of the Radical Change a rallying point (us versus *it*). Good people rise to a tough challenge, and when they pull together in their effort to surmount it, an *esprit de corps*, a sense of purpose and, yes, motivation build and eventually replace the anger, despair and hopelessness.

The power of attitude

There is an old expression that usually rates at least a chuckle when uttered in a group of managers: "The flogging will continue until morale improves." People laugh at the obvious incongruity. But it poses a question: Why should a manager care about employee morale? Because attitude influences performance. Allow me to repeat that simple but powerful truth. Attitude influences performance.

An example from outside the workplace: I chaperoned a weekend camping expedition in which my

THE AWESOME
POWER OF ATTITUDE
HAS PROFOUND
IMPLICATIONS.

oldest son and his Boy Scout troop were invited to participate in a skill-building jamboree at the West Point Military Academy, along with hundreds of other young men from up and down the eastern seaboard. For months they anticipated and planned for this exclusive event. As the spring weekend approached, fronts of bad weather came and went in the Northeast. When we arrived at West Point, skies were partly cloudy overhead and the ground was mostly muddy underfoot. We unpacked our gear, strapped on our backpacks and began the hike to the staging area known as Bull Hill. By the time we arrived to our appointed campsite on the steep slope of a wide-open meadow, we found the sky darkening, the wind picking up and our boots quickly becoming covered with the gooey brown ooze of the mud-covered ground. As we began unpacking and preparing to set up camp, the sky let loose with the rain it could no longer hold back. The pent-up winds whipped across that open field. Within minutes, we were soaked, chilled and up to our knees in slippery slime.

Once that rain started, it never stopped. The hill we were to call "home" for the next three days immediately began eroding, giving way with every slip-slide stride we tried to take. Quickly, we abandoned all hope of respite from the rain or relief from the cold, ubiquitous mud. Against the odds, we staked our flimsy shelters to that moving mass of mud. We laid out our sleeping bags in the mud, ate in the mud, traveled to the latrine in the mud and finally, on that cold, wet Friday night, slept in the mud.

At 5:30 the next morning, revelry blew. Within minutes after we put on our cold, mud-filled boots, emerged from our wet tents and stepped into a muck that grabbed our feet and refused to let go, a commotion rang through our camp-pitched-on-the-slope. Young army cadets were gathering and herding the slightly younger scouts for a rain-drenched round of early morning calisthenics. "Let's go! Up and at 'em!" they enthused. Now, up until this point, we accompanying adults did all we could to keep the kids from demanding an immediate about-face and retreat from their chilly, slimy, sinking encampment. I could not imagine those kids going into the cold morning rain before sunrise to exercise in the mud. Still, with the naiveté of youth, they followed their cheerful cadet leaders to the bottom of the hill and began calling off repetitions in military cadence. I followed our boys, prepared to drag back the wounded (and any who at the last minute declared themselves conscientious objectors). After essentially crawling to the assigned spot at the bottom of the hill, the boys met their gung-ho leaders. In a loud, chipper tone, the cadets urged the boys to engage in what, given the conditions, could feel only like self-abuse. To my utter surprise, with this bit of encouragement from those high-energy soldiers, those chilled-to-the-bone, mud-infested, sleep-deprived scouts got down and started doing push-ups in the mud. The infectious chant, "Are you motivated? Are you motivated? Are you motivated?" had a strange way of helping those kids overcome true physical discomfort to perform strenuous acts under miserable conditions that

129

I could not imagine anyone subjecting themselves to willingly. Attitude influences performance.

The knowledge/psyche/motivation triad

In today's workplace, the awesome power of attitude has profound implications. When employees merely perform basic tasks (screw this nut on that bolt), how they feel about their work is of consequence perhaps only to the extent that it influences the speed at which they work or the length of their endurance. However, the work your organization produces is most likely based much more on knowledge and service. In this environment, an employee's attitude—how he or she feels about his or her work—affects the quality of the work produced.

Knowledge work is the product of ideas. Service work is largely the product of personality. Ideas and personality are both tied to one's mental state. Frustrated, bored and angry knowledge workers don't think like those who enjoy a more positive frame of mind. Likewise, frustrated, bored and angry service personnel don't treat customers in the same way as if they were pleased with their employer and felt a sense of purpose and joy in their work.

Morale counts; if it didn't, how could there be a "morale problem"? Morale matters. CEOs and other senior execs of companies I consult with often confide that they just can't get their middle managers and other employees to commit all their energy to the business. In essence, they ask, "How can I get employees to care as much about the business as I do?" I like to respond by asking a question of my own: "Why should they care any more than enough to stay on the payroll?" If an organization's management asks me to motivate their employees, I am very suspicious. Often, what they really want is a secret method to get their employees to do work they really don't want to do or to do it in a way they'd rather not. No speech, slogan or pep rally is going to make that happen!

Here's why the relationship between an individual's emotional state and his or her work product is so important: Greatness, meeting the challenges created by Radical Change with inspired work, comes from people who are motivated to give much more thinking, creativity and energy than merely fulfilling the requirements of their job descriptions. These are matters of heart and soul. And heart and soul are never for sale, so they cannot be bought; they must be freely given. Attempting to require or trade for inspired work is like trying to force seeds to grow. If you tried to barter for greater participation and contribution in the newly changed organization, you wouldn't have much to put on the bargaining table. For what are employees exchanging their hard work? A short-term gain? A long-term gain? Job security? A secure pension? Richer benefits? More time off? The prospect of promotion? A way to avoid immediate dismissal?

While a person's loyalty and commitment to meeting your organization's challenges cannot be purchased, you as a Value-adding Manager can help to create the conditions in which an employee is more

131

The Commitment Continuum
Attitudes Drive Actions

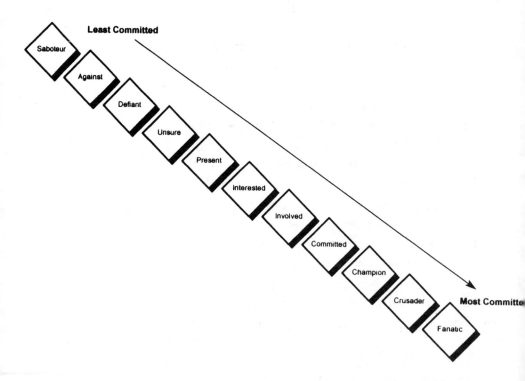

likely to give you the most precious parts of his or her creative self. As pointed out in Chapter 4, your personal relationship with your employees as their immediate boss exerts the greatest influence on how they feel about working for your organization. A quiet acknowledgment of that is heard in the way people talk about their reporting relationships in an organization. Tom Smith, who reports to Jane Doe, is said to be "working for" Ms. Doe. While the difference in semantics may seem subtle, it's significant. This "working for" concept speaks volumes about the power of the personal relationship between boss and direct reports. A boss's personal credibility is more important than his or her organizational authority. That credibility helps to inspire personal loyalty, which in turn plays a big role in inspiring employees to deliver high performance under lowly conditions. (In a similar vein, the collegial relationship between co-workers can be a strong factor in delivering performance under the adverse circumstances created by Radical Change. Employees may work hard more to help their colleagues than to help their employer, sometimes uniting against a common enemy: the institution which happens to pay them.)

As a Value-adding Manager, with the power of your sincerity and clarity of mission, you confirm to the people in your group, who are toiling away, giving of themselves and going beyond the minimum, that they are not fools but people freely making valid contributions to an important effort. Thus, in your role as boss, honest humanity is a motivator. With

THE GREATEST CHALLENGE YOU FACE AND GREATEST CONTRIBUTION YOU CAN MAKE IS TO HELP EMPLOYEES FEEL LESS LIKE INTERCHANGEABLE AND DISPOSABLE PARTS.

133

apologies to Erich Segal, effectively leading people means being able to say "thank you" and "I'm sorry." The power of this simple truth may be best evidenced by a stunning example of its opposite. One of my corporate responsibilities is to administer my organization's annual incentive trip for a select few employees to a sun-drenched exotic port. The prospect of attending, with one's spouse or guest, this celebratory and fun affair—complete with all meals, entertainment and recreation fully company-paid—is a real motivator for top achievers. One year, a few weeks before the upcoming dream event to be held in the warm and picturesque U.S. Virgin Islands during the dark deep-freeze of January, I received a disturbing call from a manager who won the trip. With great conviction in her voice, she told me she would not attend the celebration in the Caribbean. "I'm going to resign instead," she proclaimed. "I refuse to attend...as a protest against the power-hungry dictator I've been working for."

Now, this manager certainly could have accepted the trip, ate, drank and been merry on the company tab and then resigned. But she felt so strongly that she wanted to make as bold a statement as possible. And in the process she provided so important a lesson to anyone who would hear her story. Tangible rewards, no matter how attractive, do not substitute or compensate for honorable, humane treatment by a person's boss. (By the way, Mr. Power, this manager's boss, did attend the party in the Caribbean. He was dismissed about a year later during a corporate reorganization.)

In today's corporate environment, the greatest challenge you face, and the greatest contribution you can make as a manager, is to help employees to feel less like interchangeable and disposable parts and more like unique human contributors whom you respect, trust and value.

The 3Rs of motivation and other secrets

How do you communicate to the people you lead that you are worth following beyond the path of least resistance and down a road of difficult challenges? There are three primary factors in sustaining an environment that encourages employees to go above and beyond the job description. You might think of these as the 3Rs of motivation:

- Responsibility.
- Recognition.
- Reward.

Responsibility

Giving your employees clear accountability for their work and expected outcomes gives meaning to their investment of self. Without that accountability, they are mere cogs in a machine controlled by someone else. What is the difference, then, between great or mediocre performance? A key element of accountability is *choice*. When someone chooses to accept responsibility, they have willingly invested

135

themselves in the outcomes. Without a choice, accountability becomes a veil for coercion. How can you make accepting responsibility for results a choice? By making clear to your employees that they have an option to accept or reject the responsibility. This may seem especially difficult when you are struggling with a smaller staff following Radical Change. But the principle applies regardless of the size of your staff or the degree to which they are burdened. For responsibility to be a meaningful motivator for great results, it must be freely chosen.

HEART AND SOUL ARE NEVER FOR SALE, SO THEY CANNOT BE BOUGHT; THEY MUST BE FREELY GIVEN.

To be certain the choice is one made without pressure, offer an attractive alternative, say, a generous severance package that doesn't unduly penalize someone for choosing not to accept the responsibility they really aren't ready for. Otherwise, you've backed your employee into a corner where they are not only unmotivated but condemned to fail. Conversely, once ownership of responsibility is freely assumed, woe to anyone who stands in the employee's way of producing great results; the employee dictates the methods as well as the results. One of the great excuses for failing to perform to expectation, one that you just might be forced to accept, is this: "I was doing exactly what you told me to do."

There is no power like the one that you instill when you say to an employee, "This is yours. Make it the best it can be." Say that, then get out of the way. Stand back, and watch great things unfold before your eyes.

Recognition

While personal ownership of one's work is rewarding in and of itself, it's made even more potent when you as a Value-adding Manager adopt an attitude of gratitude for a job well done. Recognizing good work says to the employee that you noticed the effort and that he or she was neither foolish nor abused for the extra hard work it took to produce the outcome. I've seen many six-figure executives, who earned bonuses for delivering their target goals, sulk because they felt that, despite the money, their boss didn't fully appreciate their achievements. In a poll by the American Productivity and Quality Center in Houston, Texas, more than 90 percent of the employees it surveyed said that "recognition when I've done a job well" is important or very important in motivating them. Feeling underappreciated is common; employees surveyed by the American Productivity and Quality Center reported that while their bosses were giving them autonomy on the job (85 percent rated their supervisor as good or excellent at leaving them alone), they were not so good at giving regular feedback on performance. Only 32 percent said their boss was good or excellent on that account. And consistent with numerous surveys since the 1940s, employees continue to rank recognition as a stronger motivator than either "competitive salary" or "pay clearly tied to performance." Recognition matters; recognition motivates.

Taking a moment to say, "Thanks for a job well done," costs nothing and can pay huge dividends in morale and in encouraging future performance. So why do so many bosses so rarely express their appreciation for the work of their employees? Some of them believe they are encouraging good work when they aren't critical of the people who report to them. Make no mistake: The absence of criticism isn't the same as recognition. No one mistakes the boss's silence for approval or appreciation.

The reason so many bosses apparently fail to recognize their employees is due not to the expense of time or energy required to say thanks, but to something that many bosses find totally inhibiting: giving credit where credit is due.

Blohowiak's Law of Organizational Accountability states: "Credit for any job well done flows to the highest level in the organization possible; blame for any error or failure sinks to the lowest level possible."

When you give credit where credit is due—especially if it goes to people whose function or employment class wouldn't ordinarily bring them much attention—you say something to the people you rightfully recognize. You also say much more about yourself: that you are a decent, trustworthy human being.

Willingly giving credit is but one half of the recipe for effective recognition. The other half is *how* you give credit. Have you ever attended an awards ceremony at which the presenter reluctantly came forward and mumbled something like, "Well, HR says I'm supposed to give out these plaques and things," and then proceeded to call out names with all the warmth of a drill sergeant?

The power of recognition lies in the linkage between the employee's good work and your effective acknowledgment of it, tying together the organization's goals and values, the employee's accomplishment, your gratitude and the device you're using to express it (plaque, prize, pay).

Effective recognition is overt, intentional and most importantly, specific to results delivered. Anything less doesn't count. Example: I bought a pair of glasses at a national chain store, and as I was paying the bill, I noticed the picture of my helpful sales clerk on a plaque hanging over the register proclaiming, "Employee of the Month!" "Hey, Tom, good for you!" I said. "Tell me, what did you do to deserve that?" Tom looked at me sheepishly. In a low whisper, he said, "To tell you the truth, I have no idea." Not wanting to embarrass poor, confused Tom, I joked, "Well, keep it up anyway!" We both laughed at the unfortunate position Tom's well-intending employer had put him in. With a little preparation and ceremony, Tom's boss could have clearly tied Tom's obvious qualities of patience, care and sales skills to the publicity he was to receive from having his likeness stare out at all customers paying their bills.

How to say 'thanks' in a meaningful and memorable way

Here's a simple six-step process for effectively extending recognition in either a public or private session to a deserving employee:

139

1. Describe the relevant part of the organization's mission (goals for quality, revenues, cost-cutting, etc.).

2. Specify how the person or group you're recognizing helped to meet those organizational goals by exemplary performance (meeting or beating an ambitious deadline, delivering results under difficult circumstances, inventing new solutions to vexing challenges). Work in some personal anecdotes to show that you were paying attention to the individual effort behind the achievement.

3. Distinguish the results (more satisfied customers, improved profits, reduced waste or expenses) from the effort. The more specific you can be, the more credence your recognition carries.

4. Express your personal appreciation and make the connection between the efforts, the results and your organization's values (as contrasted with goals, which you've already mentioned).

5. Relate the award to the achievement, pointing out the symbolic significance of the award you are bestowing upon the recipient ("This award is named for so-and-so who…"; "The design of this crystal star represents…"; "This gift certificate for a nice dinner out recognizes that you gave up a lot of your free time to produce…").

6. Then tie the award to its commemorative nature, implying that it does not represent payment for the achievement but rather an extension of the recognition ceremony ("So, Jane, I hope every time you glance up at this framed certificate, it reminds you of our gathering tonight and of the deep appreciation that American Amalgamated feels for what you've done...").

Present the recognition device with a smile, a warm handshake and a personal "thank you."

Reward

When thinking of rewards, you might automatically think of monetary compensation. Money can be validating, but it is not necessarily motivating, particularly when base salary is considered. Salary becomes an irrevocable entitlement. Upon having attained a comfortable salary level, an individual may think, *This is what I'm worth; this is what I deserve.*

However, when the promise of a specific reward is tied to the attainment of specific results, money can be a great motivator—provided the individual who is supposed to be incited by the reward truly wants it and is willing to do what is necessary to earn it.

Some people confuse rewards, incentives and bribes. They are easily distinguishable. A reward compensates for results produced ("You're receiving this bonus for producing the project to spec, on time and within budget."). An incentive is the promise to give someone a reward for delivering specified

WITHOUT INCENTIVES AND REWARDS, THE ONLY CONSEQUENCES FOR RISK-TAKING ONE CAN IMAGINE ARE NEGATIVE.

141

results; it is conditional ("You'll receive this bonus providing you produce the project to spec, on time and within budget."). A bribe attempts to influence someone to take actions that violate a position of trust in exchange for something of value ("I'm giving you this money today so you'll name me as your vendor next week even though my company didn't meet your quality standard.").

At a cocktail party I attended, a minister who had read some of my writings on the subject of rewards confronted me. "You cost me a hundred dollars today!" he said accusingly. Stunned, I groped to understand how I possibly could have caused this man of the cloth to part with his money. "After reading what you wrote about rewarding people for their good work, I felt so guilty that I wanted to give my secretary something extra for all her hard work on a major project we just completed." I took this good-natured ribbing from the good reverend as validation from a higher authority that there is nothing untoward about rewarding people for a job well done or letting them know in advance that you consider it more valuable for them to meet specific objectives than not to meet them.

Some people challenge the idea that an incentive can positively affect knowledge workers' creativity or work performance. While it may be self-evident that the promise of a monetary or other tangible reward won't in and of itself cause someone to be smarter, more ingenious or collaborative, it's equally obvious that this fact isn't a reason to deny knowledge workers incentives. The promise of paying more for desirable results certainly can encourage someone to work harder on an assignment and to put more time and energy into a project instead of other endeavors that might be more fun but less rewarding. With proper incentives, I'm probably more inclined to spend a bit more time reviewing research or reconfiguring my project's numbers at the expense of more golfing or moviegoing than if there were no consequences at stake.

The beauty of incentives and rewards is that they make clear the relationship between results and compensation; this relationship becomes increasingly important in the intensely competitive marketplace. Rewards provide a reason to circumvent this seemingly immutable law of nature: Most people seek the lowest possible risk level. Rewards and incentives encourage going out on a limb for results because there's a payoff for success. Without incentives and rewards, the only consequences for risk-taking one can imagine are negative.

Because Radical Change has trimmed the number of people contributing to an organization's success, I believe strongly that everyone — at all levels — should have some of their compensation determined by results. Results could be anything from revenues, profits, customer satisfaction ratings and quality measures to cycle time reduction, a consistent safety record, new dealers or stores carrying your product — anything that is a measurable result. The portion of an individual's income that is variable (and therefore at risk) should depend on two factors: the size of his or her base salary and the degree of influence he or

143

she exerts over the results for which that individual is being compensated. Someone in the mailroom does make a contribution to overall sales results but not to the extent the VP of sales does. (See the performance management section ahead.)

Despite the power of incentives to bring about behavior that drives positive results, the volatile nature of the new organization may limit the effect incentives have on performance. In a place rocked by Radical Change, even very senior people may wonder, "Will I stay on the payroll long enough to collect?"

ATTITUDE
INFLUENCES
PERFORMANCE.

Money, of course, is but the most common form of reward. Rewards come in both tangible forms (bonuses, trips, prizes) and symbolic forms (Olympic medals, Nobel and Pulitzer prizes, Employee-of-the-Year plaques). Some people question whether symbolic rewards do much to influence behavior. Some of these same people battle like hell to win golf trophies at their conventions or push for the biggest office with the tallest windows and plushest carpets. Monetary rewards make a temporary and easily forgotten dent on one's bank account while symbolic rewards make a lasting and indelible emotional impression. When employees are rewarded with both tangible and symbolic rewards, they are provided with potent reinforcers that encourage continued achievement.

The most powerful symbolic reward I know is the "refrigerator letter." (For descriptions of others, see my books *Mavericks!* and *Lead Your Staff to Think Like Einstein, Create Like da Vinci and Invent*

Like Edison.) The refrigerator letter is a personal note of thanks that you write to an employee at the completion of a job well done. Instead of sending it through e-mail or interoffice mail, you mail it to the employee's home. What happens next is this: After opening and reading the letter, passing out from shock and traumatic disbelief, recovering and showing the appreciative note to a skeptical mate, the recipient of the letter posts it (under a little magnetized cow or chicken) on the refrigerator, where friends and family review it with total surprise and deep admiration. "You know, honey," says the now proud spouse, "even though I'd rather have you here at home, I'm darn glad they noticed your 80-hour workweeks. I always knew you had the right stuff."

Managers are people, too

If you have managers reporting to you, are you ignoring them in the recognition department? It's easy to neglect managers, especially when they're competent and busy filling vacuums created by Radical Change. Even self-motivated managers can benefit from a little extra fuel for their fire. Make a point of telling your managers that you're aware of and appreciate the fine work they're doing. Not only will it spur them on, but it will likely encourage them to say something affirming to the people who report to them. That's the power of leading by example.

Vendors are people, too

With the trend to outsourcing, you may have
people you work with day in and day out who are
not on your company's payroll but are, technically,
vendors. Well, regardless of from whose bank
account their paychecks are drawn, these people are
working for you. The same positive power of recognition that can motivate your staff applies to your
vendors.

Business is nothing more than relationships between people in which money is involved. Results
are usually best when as much emphasis is placed on
the relationships as on the money.

Performance management systems

Does your organization still require the yearly
merit review (sometimes affectionately referred to as
the annual sneak attack)? Everyone I know, on both
sides of the desk, dreads these things and for good
reason. The employee is subjected to what seems like
arbitrary judgment, and the manager is forced to sit
in the seat of judgment and make decisions that bear
directly on another human being's livelihood and
career. It's an important and weighty responsibility,
not to be taken lightly; nonetheless, every day scores
of employees are subjected to unfair and unfounded
"reviews" by unprepared supervisors.

Development Dimensions International and
the Society for Human Resource Management
sponsored a survey of more than 1,100 employees

and found numerous frustrations with performance assessments. The gripes at the top of the list were:

- Performance management is a once-a-year event with no periodic reviews.
- Employees have little opportunity for involvement in their assessments.
- Rewards received are not appropriate to performance delivered.
- Bosses are biased or inconsistent in their ratings.

Some managers, suffering an acute case of guilt for not having kept good records of their observations, surrender to an impulse to endow the employee with "the benefit of the doubt." In this case, that means the boss doubts he or she could defend anything other than a most generalized review and so fills in the narrative with empty phrases like "meets most job requirements" and "shows steady progress." Then, to conclude this little charade, the boss recommends giving the employee in question a slightly above average (wouldn't want to discourage anyone!) annual raise because there was no evidence to make a case against doing so. Unfortunately, effect without cause cannot influence future behavior. When pay increases appear automatic, employees soon get this message: Mere endurance for another 12 months is the basis for earning another increase to base salary. And doing nothing more than what is required to stay employed or doing it with a bit more finesse really makes no difference when it comes to divvying the

147

pay pie. Mediocrity is perfectly acceptable and well compensated here—all without the bother of accountability.

If you simply want to keep employees even with inflation, call the raise an inflation adjustment. That's at least clear and honest.

An alternative to automatic increases to base salary is a performance bonus system. Central to this compensation approach is a requirement to truly discriminate between employees in terms of the relative value each contributed. The reward may be strictly a one-time bonus or a combination of bonus and adjustment to base salary. (Obviously, the smaller the increases to salary, the less your fixed costs increase.)

To make a true performance-based system work, view performance expectations and evaluations as having three components:

1. The work that must be done to basically fulfill the job (the "job description" part of the job and any specific goals mutually agreed upon by you and the employee).

2. How the work was performed (cooperatively, on time, within budget).

3. The unique added-value deliverables the person filling the position brought to it (e.g., new projects tackled by own initiative, cost savings, suggested ways to shave time or increase quality).

In reviewing performance, you must consider all three components. A self-motivated employee who shines in the unique added-value department, dreaming up and working on nifty projects while failing to complete basic job responsibilities, hasn't fulfilled fundamental expectations and shouldn't be rewarded as though he or she had.

The reality underpinning a reward program that discriminates between employees is this: There is a limited amount of money to be distributed to people on the payroll. The justification for unequal rewards must be based on measurable outcomes, but measurable outcomes cannot be the only standard. Behaviors may be as (or more) important than results. A tyrant can, in the short-term, extract results through fear and abuse; a crook can log gains by misrepresentation or deploying kickbacks or other ethically depraved methods. Compensation must consider both the right means and the right ends. Those receiving performance bonuses should excel at both.

The power of meaning

Some management pundits suggest that "what gets rewarded gets done." This implies that employees' behavior is most influenced by favors extended by their managers. The image that springs to my mind is that of a trainer saying, "Roll over. Good dog! Here's a treat." Undeniably, reinforcing desirable results with external rewards plays a part in encouraging similar performance in the future. But to suggest, as some have, that "what gets rewarded gets done" is equivalent to the greatest management principle in the world is to view motivation as an

THE TIME OF ONE'S LIFE IS LITERALLY SPENT AT WORK.

149

exercise in manipulation. It's not "what gets rewarded gets done"; rather, it's "what's rewarding gets done."

The time of one's life is literally spent at work. We spend more time on the job than with a significant other, loved ones, enjoying hobbies, volunteering or recreating in all other ways. With that much of your life devoted to one thing, don't you want it to have some meaning, to be something other than a waste of your precious time? Whether consciously aware of it or not, most everyone has the same need. In fact, a Gallup Poll of American workers in 1991 reported this fascinating insight into the psychology of work: 78 percent of the respondents said that "interesting work" was very important to them, while only 56 percent said that a "high income" was.

"Meaning on the job" can come from the work itself (especially if it makes the world a better place), but it can also come from the pride of working for one's organization—feeling part of something special and important. Consider this: A representative of a major supplier of company "service awards" (gifts given to employees to mark their employment anniversaries at 5, 10 and 25 years) told me that some employers give their employees a choice as to whether they want to receive their clocks, pens and other commemorative items with or without the company's logo. Fully 76 percent of the service awards that can be ordered without a logo are ordered *with* one. People derive pleasure from their association with the organization in which they invest so much of themselves.

This works both ways. While being part of the corporate society is rewarding, the benefits of belonging are lessened when the society becomes more unstable as it's rocked by Radical Change. The personal relationships people once enjoyed in their workplace become more distant and less familiar as they come to understand that their (or their friends') participation in this corporate society could be severed in an instant without warning.

Another measure of the import of emotional fulfillment in the workplace: When someone feels that they truly need to leave a job, offering them more money usually won't change their decision or turn their dissatisfaction into delight. People leave jobs when they have no sense of contribution or feel that their contribution is undervalued in terms of tangible or intangible rewards. Contribution and accomplishment are a job's greatest rewards, more valued than money but not substitutes for it.

I once worked for a boss who challenged her employees with this suggestion: "Ask yourself, 'Am I in this job for something to do or to do something?' " She wanted to surround herself with people who wanted to do something, to make a meaningful contribution (people who wanted to build a hospital, not merely lay bricks). That kind of motivation is internally driven; as a Value-adding Manager you can foster it, cheer it and reward it when appropriate. With the right employees and their thoughtful support, you'll have a team motivated by pride, care and quality doing great work. And that's something to cheer about.

Chapter 8

Destroying obstacles to greatness: Leader as dragon slayer

If change means giving birth to something new, the price of change is the death of its predecessor. In an organization, this truth is a painful one, one that carries obligations for the leaders of that organization. Leadership implicitly means driving change, for no one leads people to where they already are.

A Value-adding Manager must continually be dissatisfied with what is, always searching for better ways of getting the job done and continually redefining what the job is. This means assuming the role of the dragon slayer, the brave, naked soul who willfully (if not terribly willingly) takes on dangerous and powerful beasts, some of which may be frighteningly close to home.

THE AUTHENTIC LEADER IS A TRADITION KILLER.

To say you "institutionalize change" may seem to be an oxymoron. But wrapped within that paradox is an imperative task you must fulfill when you presume to lead in today's organization.

153

FEBA

A colleague of mine, Scott, is a graduate of the West Point Military Academy. One day we were joking about (belittling, actually) business buzzwords and acronyms. I pushed him for some West Point acronyms, knowing full well that the military is the "grandest acronym creator of all," or "GACA." After a few minutes, Scott came up with FEBA, Forward Edge of the Battle Area. This, I thought, held great promise as a fashionable business buzzword. And so, against my personal credo, I shall use this buzzwordy term to make a point.

As a Value-adding Manager, you are an agent, a champion of Radical Change, a combatant at the forward edge of the battle area. You must constantly work to create a new present that destroys the unproductive vestiges of the past. In this role, you can hold nothing sacred, especially anything you've created or fallen in love with. Recognize and overcome any reluctance to tear down what you built, after shaking off the paralysis that grips you when you realize you must destroy something you worked hard to build.

A benign and unthreatening circumstance in my personal life recently demonstrated this need to cling to the past. While my wife, Susan, and I have moved around the country several times in pursuit of the economic brass ring, she has always done far more packing and preparing for those moves than I have. I was (gently) reminded of this in a recent move across town. In preparing for this move, I seemed to take forever to accomplish as simple a task as packing the contents of my desk drawers. During the time it took me to pack a few pencils, paperweights and miscellaneous doodads, Susan had packed every dish, glass and kitchen utensil, as well as the clothes in four closets and the many volumes in our book collection. Not being a shirker, I was amazed to discover my pitiful productivity. Upon reflection, I discovered why I was poky. Even though I very much wanted to move to our new house, I clung to the familiar because it was familiar. I resisted "undoing" even for the promise of a much more comfortable future.

This same phenomenon can grip you like a straightjacket in your organization because the stakes are much higher and the possible outcomes not nearly as pleasant as moving to a new house. The upshot of your "improvements" may be to separate good, hard-working people from their livelihoods and friends or to cause confusion, upheaval and disarray in the name of progress. This takes resolve, guts and the capacity to withstand occasionally restless nights. Most importantly, it requires you to keep your sense of purpose—the greater good that results from a stronger organization—squarely in mind. This is easy to write about and understand; it is much harder to put into practice. Because challenging the system that supports a comfortable environment for you and your colleagues is difficult, making a point of critically examining everything that has worked well in the past is all the more necessary. Danger lurks where it's most comfortable and seemingly successful.

One way to avoid the inertia that accompanies the familiar is to schedule reexaminations of your operations. Take out a calendar and a pen, and set a date with yourself to question specific parts of your operation. If you don't do this, you'll do nothing more than agree that "someday" you should take a fresh, hard look at the way things are. As with starting a program to lose those extra pounds you've always intended to shed, someday never seems to come. Commit to it and follow through with it. As you begin your assessment of your operation, avoid falling into the pit of "Restructuring Lite": looking at your operation and making plans to radically change it with the same commitment I brought to packing my desk drawers. Swallow hard, steel your nerve and question everything—without regard for tradition, personal preference or personnel. This is as hard and ugly as it is necessary. This process places the forward edge of the battle area about dead-even with your belly button.

MANAGER-AS-HERO IS A GRATIFYING BUT DEBILITATING CONDITION.

Dragons to slay

The job of creating and managing change is the job of slaying dragons. They come in many forms and require a Value-adding Manager to wield a varied arsenal. The most important arrow in the dragon slayer's quiver is courage. In the go-go-go age of Radical Change, courage must increasingly overcome correctness.

It is necessary to occasionally challenge not just your colleagues but your boss and the company's chief executive. Even the best-run organizations make errors in their strategy or tactics. Silence is the coconspirator of misguided deeds.

You have an obligation to challenge policies and programs not in the organization's best interest. That requires courage (or a communications channel that accepts anonymous messages). It also takes courage to confront, and even fire, results-delivering jerks, like a manager who exceeds corporate goals but who's unfair to minorities, a male employee who's impolite to women or a member of your staff who takes credit for others' work.

As a dragon slayer, you have a right to righteous anger. Like the kind that boils up when you see someone working with flagrant disregard for quality, reneging on a commitment or not pulling a fair share of the load. Or the anger you feel over compensation programs that are inadequate or corporate goals that are inadequately supported. Or wasteful excesses by self-pampering top executives who don't live by the constraints they decree for others. When you feel righteous anger welling up, channel it. If you're in a position where it's appropriate for you to take action, act. If you can't take direct action, talk or send a note to someone who can effect positive change and right the wrongs. If you are truly not able to influence the source of your anger, come to terms with the situation and channel your energy into something within your control. Use the force of your emotions to effect positive change in some fashion.

157

Unearth and destroy bureaucracy at every opportunity. Bureaucracy smothers, chokes and strangles innovation. Question rules, forms and policies. Of every stricture that slows work down, ask, "Is it necessary? What's the risk of eliminating it?" If the risk is minimal, abolish the rule. Don't hamper 98 percent of your people with rules designed to govern a wayward 2 percent. That 2 percent ignores rules anyway. Set your people free.

Slay the dragons that constitute the triple threat to positive change:

- "We've always done it this way."
- "We've never done it that way."
- "We tried that once." (The fiercest dragon of them all.)

The greatest dragon of all

There are many dragons to slay and demons to wrestle with, but the mightiest dragons are those within. Aristotle wrote, "The hardest victory is victory over self." Everyone has dragons inside: habits, fears, experiences that color judgment. Because these dragons are hidden on the inside, they might be the most difficult to recognize. And the most important to slay.

Here are some garden-variety internal dragons that need slaying:

Habits. To save time and become consistent, you probably have many routines to shortcut through

Short Take: Firing Miss Little People

I have always found firing people, even people who clearly needed to be separated from the organization, to be stressful. The night before I was to do the deed was usually one with little sleep. With one exception.

Following a corporate reorganization, I inherited a manager who made a handsome salary. When she was assigned to my group, I wanted to give this manager every opportunity to make a contribution. We had some prior dealings but not enough for me to have formed an opinion of her capabilities. I invited her to lunch to discuss her role in our changing company.

We hadn't finished our salads when it became clear to me that we had what some people euphemistically describe as a "difference in management philosophy." I probably could have tolerated her inflated sense of experience and capabilities. But what I absolutely bristled at was her penchant for describing other members of her new work group as "worker bees" and "the little people." Her obvious disdain for her new colleagues was as unmistakable as it was repugnant.

Long before I finished my entrée, I made the decision to cut short the misery this manager would undoubtedly inflict upon her fellow employees. Immediately upon arriving back at the office, I started the paperwork necessary to quickly separate this arrogant person from an organization that clearly had no place for her.

When the administrative hurdles had been cleared, I set an appointment for the following day to again meet with Miss Little People. That night, I slept soundly, restfully and peacefully. I cannot say I took joy in the experience of firing her, but I can say I never regretted it.

everyday tasks. Think of this repetition as a path. Every time you go down that path, you wear it deeper. With repeated use time after time, deeper and deeper it gets until eventually the path is a rut and finally a pit. The path you took to make you more efficient and productive turns into a trap from which you can see no alternatives. You trade convenience for creativity, expedience for perspective. Practice makes permanent (not perfect), so make no habits.

Ego. A strong sense of self likely has been an important ingredient in your success formula. You're in a managerial spot in a post-Radical Change organization because you're good at what you do. And to get better, to be more effective, you'll likely have to do less of what you do. What I'm talking about here is letting go of your "manager as hero" role. When you're in your hero role, your whole staff can be stumped, stymied, up against the wall trying to solve a problem, undo a wrong or make sense of confusing or conflicting data. Enter you, the wise, experienced, tested-by-fire executive. Just when it seems time to abandon all hope, you swoop down like Batman coming to save Gotham City. Pow! Wham! Bam! Problem solved. You feel great having worked your magic yet once again. Your staff is in awe…and no more capable than they were before. Manager-as-hero is a gratifying but debilitating condition. Slay this dragon. It prevents your staff from growing in capabilities and forces you to take time away from higher value work to fight fires you shouldn't even know exist.

The next time your staff calls for help, guide them to find their own way out but don't rush to the Batmobile. A great way to develop your staff and yourself, while scoring points with your boss, is to use the double delegation technique. This is a gem I picked up from my friend, magazine publisher Morrie Helitzer. He suggests making a list of all your tasks and responsibilities. Then review the list to identify those things that you do that members of your staff could also do. Delegating offers your staff growth opportunities while providing you with an opportunity to take advantage of the second half of the double delegation, which is to make a list of what your boss currently does that you could do. Offering to help your boss free up his or her workload by picking up certain obligations is a way of enlarging your challenges and responsibilities and helping your poor, overworked colleague get a needed break. (This might be a real "win-win-win" for you, your staff and your boss.)

Fears. Everyone is afraid of something. In the age of Radical Change, fears we didn't know we had come bubbling up. Like the fear of being disposable to an organization you long believed loved you. Like the fear that a capable staff may make you unnecessary. Sound far-fetched? Here's a case in point. One summer's day, I was signing autographs at a large bookstore for a book that promised to teach managers to have a staff that was far more capable, creative and inventive. I was standing near the store entrance behind a display with a bright spotlight shining down on a large poster of the book. A middle-aged man stopped, read the book's title, *Lead Your Staff to Think Like Einstein, Create Like da Vinci and Invent Like Edison*, looked me in the eye and said, "Ha! Why would anyone want to have a staff like that?!" I laughed at the man's apparent joke. But he wasn't kidding. He went on to explain that he had lost his managerial job with a large company "after teaching my people everything I knew. The thanks for my trouble was to get fired." After the

A SELF-SUFFICIENT STAFF IS NOT SOMETHING TO FEAR BUT TO STRIVE FOR.

gentleman left the store (empty-handed, as you might expect), I thought long and hard about his challenge. Two conclusions have come to me from that conversation. First, this hapless fellow's experience represents a nightmare that haunts many managers these days: The staff they carefully develop may one day serve as the very reason their boss is no longer necessary on the payroll. Second, there is no reason why this dark fear should become reality. The reason this manager lost his job after developing his staff is because he added no more value. He didn't get beyond his habits, didn't bring anything new to the table. His problem wasn't the competency of his staff, it was his competency. With the demands placed on you by the ever-higher expectations created by Radical Change, you must have the most competent and capable staff you can develop. A self-sufficient staff is not something to fear but to strive for. When your employees assume more responsibility, your role as their leader isn't diminished; in fact, it may increase as you are able to challenge your people with even tougher assignments, standards and deadlines. You can't get better as a department if your people aren't up to the challenge, and they won't be if you don't develop them. Your time is better spent educating, cheerleading and quality-assuring your staff and their activities, rather than completing or closely supervising tasks yourself—even your favorite tasks. As you give up tasks and over-the-shoulder supervisory work, you can continue developing yourself and continually add new value. You want to make a contribution so unique that when the time comes (again and again) for your organization to reevaluate its managers, you're one of those people that top management couldn't imagine not having on the payroll.

Biases. No matter how broadminded you are, you have some narrow-minded thoughts somewhere in the subconscious recesses of your brain. You harbor biases and prejudices not because you're a bad person but because you're human. I'd imagine that most senior executives would tell you they are open-minded and unbiased. So why, despite their own clear, firm corporate policies against discrimination, are so few women and minorities in positions of power? Somehow, the broad, open-minded and unbiased (white male) executives who sit in the seats of power don't seem to find a place at the table for people unlike themselves. All of us hold some biases that might subtly stand in the way of progress. Many of them concern people we don't know very well:

- "She's not right for us with that accent."
- "We don't hire people with beards."
- "His many different occupations make it clear he has no sense of a career path."
- "Our customers prefer to interact with more attractive personnel."
- "That wheelchair could be distracting to other workers."
- "We only hire college graduates."
- "A blind person couldn't keep up with the demand."

- "Gee, I'm not sure a Black man would do well in that sales territory."
- "Her sign language would slow down the group."
- "The last time we hired somebody like that, it was a disaster."

The toughest part of overcoming biases is to recognize them. You might think you're not hiring or promoting someone for logical, defensible reasons (not as much experience in this or that) when your real reservation is more emotional, prejudicial and difficult to admit. (You've never worked with someone of that description, and you're not sure if you'd be comfortable doing so.) It's hard to slay a dragon you don't know is there. Make a point of questioning yourself, trying hard to unearth hidden biases and deep-seated prejudices that could preclude your success. When you uncover beliefs or attitudes you're surprised to discover, spare yourself the guilt (most everyone is less comfortable with the unfamiliar!) and move right to an honest assessment of whether your judgment is affected by these feelings. If it is, work through the feelings to get past them. Your continued success may well depend on developing this skill.

Status and competence. Are people in a position of authority supposed to know more than the people they supervise? A dragon may lie in your answer. The height of the box one occupies on the organization chart gives no clue as to the depth of one's knowledge or potential to make a significant

YOU HAVE A RIGHT TO RIGHTEOUS ANGER.

164

contribution. Important specialized knowledge may be concentrated away from the top. A stunning example of this was demonstrated in the events leading up to the Challenger space shuttle disaster. The warnings of knowledgeable lower-level engineers were fatally overruled by top-level bureaucrats whose status exceeded their expertise. Organizational status implies nothing about competence—at either end of the hierarchy. That's why it's so important to seek insight from many quarters and listen without regard for a person's title, tenure or income. A great way to institutionalize that approach is to hold "level down" meetings with your managers' reports. In a friendly, nonthreatening conversation, get a sense of whether things are working well on the front lines. What support is missing? What unnecessary work is being done? What mixed messages are confusing people or wasting time? How valued is their input? What skill improvements do they feel they need? In other words, what have you missed by flying in the stratosphere where you can't see the details in the trenches?

Comfort. One reason Old Familiar, Inc. no longer exists is that it contentedly settled into its ways until the weight of its comfort nearly crushed it. Comfort is alluring, seductive and potentially destructive. The poet Kahlil Gibran wrote that comfort is a sneaky thing that enters your house as "a guest, and then becomes a host, and then a master." When comfort becomes your master, it does so because it pleases you, so much so that you'll aggressively protect it against forces that would disturb it. Radical

Change is such a force. Radical Change threatens the comfortable manager, who has become accustomed to the security of a steady (if not overly generous) paycheck, the familiarity of routine, orderly procedures and ample time and resources to do a job "the way it should be done." When Radical Change comes calling, the safe, secure world you learned to operate in may no longer exist, and if it does, it may not for long. Recognize comfort for what it is: appealing, mesmerizing and temporary. If you have it, enjoy it. But not too much. Understand that comfort has its price. Be prepared to trade this most attractive dragon for continued employability.

Success. To succeed literally means to follow. In days gone by, achieving success probably meant following certain customs and methods to achieve desirable results. Success, like comfort, is both deceiving and fleeting. When you believe you are successful, you are the most vulnerable. People have likened success to being "fat, dumb and happy." Hardly sounds desirable, does it? By all means, chase great ambitions, and when you snare a few, celebrate your achievements for sure. But recognize them not as the end of a process but as happy stops on a long and never-ending journey. True success comes from knowing that there is no such thing.

Only *believing* in better management. Believing that you should manage differently is but the first step in changing your behavior. It's not the same as actually *changing* the way you manage. The Value-adding Manager strives to improve and then improves by trying new things (some of which will work and some of which won't) and constantly adapting.

Finally, recognize that the worst of all dragons is believing you have none. Acknowledge your dragons, seek them and slay them.

Chapter 9

Selecting people who will make or break your career: Leader as talent scout

Of all the responsibilities you face as a manager, hiring is your most important, not only for your organization but for you personally.

During one of my organization's restructurings, every employee below the officer and director level was effectively out of a job and needed to apply for a position in the newly redesigned company. Every employee could apply for virtually any open position. The senior managers interviewed everyone in their respective parts of the organization, deciding on not only the managers who would report to them but the employees who would report to the managers. This time-intensive and emotionally draining ordeal required some senior managers to interview literally hundreds of candidates. Fortunately, this perverse process operated on a finite timetable with a clear end date for announcing the names and positions of the hundreds of job candidates.

PERSONALITY DEFINES COMPETENCE AS MUCH OR MORE THAN MERE TECHNICAL SKILLS.

When the fated day came, I gathered all my newly appointed staff for a brief welcome. I told them, "You are a handpicked group. I had my choice of many good candidates for every position in the department. I selected the very best people to take on the very difficult challenges that lie ahead. But I face those challenges confidently—knowing that you are taking them on with me. I have full faith and confidence in everyone in this room. I am betting my career on you."

If you stop to think about it, you bet your career on every person you hire. There is no decision you're likely to make that is any more important than deciding on the people who will determine whether you make your fiscal and quality goals, stay within budget, defeat difficult problems, create new opportunities and please your customers. This is especially true in an organization that has undergone a restructuring or downsizing, leaving you with a smaller staff. With fewer employees, every one of them counts more toward the organization's success. The shorter the chain, the more load each link must carry.

Aspire to hire your dream team

Though I'm not fond of comparing work groups to sports teams, they share an important principle. In sports, the team with the best players has a much better chance of winning; so too in business. My friend Ron Taddei tells of being at a conference and appearing on a panel with Alabama football great Coach Paul "Bear" Bryant (who racked up 323 wins in his college coaching career to hold the all-time record for the most Division I-A coaching victories, including bowl games). Ron asked the Bear his secret to attracting such talented assistant coaches. "That's easy," the Bear told Ron. "I only hire people smarter than me. If they're not, they can't help me."

The Value-adding Manager hires great people, and this chapter tells you how.

The competent personality

Job applicants spend much energy trying to impress a would-be employer, like you, with the details of their technical competence (usually through a resume providing a detailed record of formal schooling or training, previous positions held and the related tasks and achievements). What is neither apparent nor emphasized on the written record—or, often, in face-to-face interviews—is the personality and potential of the individual behind all those historical tidbits. When you fail to accurately grasp those elements, you fail to assess what may be the most important factors that should influence your hiring choice. We live and work in the era defined by rapid social and technological change requiring organizations to exhibit constant creativity and flexibility. Furthermore, our increasingly service-based economy requires more employees to be engaged in person-to-person contact. All these factors mean that personality defines competence as much or more than mere technical skills.

All-star traits

Employees well-equipped to deal effectively with the rigorous demands of Radical Change share certain characteristics. I'll first describe these characteristics, then give you an unusual framework for identifying them in the standard employment interview.

Initiative. Radical Change creates tremendous uncertainty—regardless of how well the organization anticipated and planned for it. The people who'll keep things running are those who don't need to be told how or when to do whatever needs to be done. They detect needs and take care of them. I call these special, wonderful people vacuum-fillers. They add value far beyond their compensation. They pay no attention to the limits of their job descriptions and work without regard for whether anyone else even notices their quiet heroics. My valued colleague and assistant Tanya is such a person, and her vacuum-filling approach to her job is to do much more than rise to the challenge of crises. A case in point: I returned to the office one morning following a business breakfast in the good old pre-Radical Change days and greeted Tanya, who asked whether I enjoyed breakfast. I told her the meeting was productive, and breakfast was extra enjoyable because I ate a wonderful new-to-me dish "called a 'friatta'—or

POTENTIAL MAY NOT BE QUANTITATIVELY MEASURABLE; HOWEVER, IT IS QUALITATIVELY ESTIMABLE.

something like that." (I wasn't quite sure of the name of this tasty omelet-like dish.) Just as quickly as I said, "Good morning," I dashed off to another meeting. When I returned, I found a yellow piece of paper on my chair. On it, Tanya had written, "Frittata: egg and vegetables." When I asked her about her little note, she explained that she went to the phone book, called an Italian restaurant and asked the chef for the correct spelling! These days, Tanya probably wouldn't have time to fill a low-value vacuum like that (the pace always seems to alternate between crisis and desperation), but she'd try. That's the way Tanya operates, filling vacuums large and small, quietly and often unexpectedly. Another case in point: When she learned that one of her colleagues had hired a college intern, Tanya quietly and by her own initiative arranged for a phone extension, a full complement of office supplies, a nameplate and myriad other amenities to make our newest addition to the group feel welcome and immediately prepared to make a contribution.

When you've hired a whole staff like Tanya, people who instinctively take care of little things when times are normal and stable, you don't need to worry about whether they'll attend to pressing matters when the whole world seems ready to fall apart around you.

Collaboration. The kind of vacuums created by Radical Change often require more than one person to fill them, no matter how enterprising the individuals on your staff. That means you need people who comfortably, naturally and apolitically pull together with others to meet challenges without concern for credit. The ideal employee blends together an ethic of valuing other people, strong, effective communication skills and a knack for working closely with others under tight deadlines and stressful conditions. While it's immensely popular to talk about "teamwork," individuals who can pull together effectively with their colleagues when the heat is on are people who are truly selfless, not selfish.

Commitment to task and results. One trait that makes vacuum-fillers vacuum-fillers is an unwavering sense of responsibility for getting the job done right. When you're really under the gun, the last thing you have energy or time to do is worry about whether your group is as dedicated as you are to producing whatever you need to produce. People with an innate resolve to see things through to completion—no matter the circumstances—don't need to be bribed, shamed or scared into doing it. I want people who want autonomy, responsibility and accountability.

Stamina. Radical Change often means working a nonstop marathon punctuated by hard sprints. There's more work than time, more pressure than relief, more expectations than means. You need people who are physically, emotionally and spiritually up to the challenge. Those up to the challenge have an iron will and physical endurance; the tougher things get, the more vigor and perseverance they muster.

Honesty. People who are honest live comfortably with truth. They're genuine, know who they are and accept themselves; they live and work with integrity. They're fair with their colleagues and their organization because that's their nature; you can always expect an honest day's work from them. They live straight, work straight and talk straight—telling you the way things really are even when it's not what you want to hear. They'll always give at least what you've asked for and let you know when they legitimately can do no more.

Resiliency. The old saying puts it in raw terms: Whatever doesn't kill you makes you stronger. Perhaps no well-adjusted person actually welcomes hardship, but those with strong coping skills are not daunted by it. Good people are like trampolines: When pushed, they use the energy to come bouncing back.

Passion. The best people care—for the business, their functional responsibilities and life. A friend who retired from the *Wall Street Journal* quotes a former colleague there as looking for employees who exhibit "organized motion"—an enthusiasm for life in all its splendor. Hire people who are passionate about something. Passionate people are intense people. The word "passion" comes from a Latin root word that literally means "to suffer." At times, passionate people may seem to care so much they hurt. And that's because they do.

Learning propensity. You need people on your staff who can quickly adapt to changing circumstances and who will figure out the alchemy to turn a mess into success. They may have significant formal education or next to none. They are people who view mistakes as their teachers and life as their classroom, who relish an opportunity to try new things and who are intrigued by the curious and fascinated by the unfamiliar. To them, a good day is one that offered a discovery or the promise of one.

Independent thinker. Those who defer to structure and authority require them and are constrained by them. Those who question, challenge and disbelieve hold the promise of innovation, improvement and excellence. A little friction with the system may generate occasional sparks, the kind that can light a fire of greatness. Interestingly, a common sign of this bent is a witty sense of humor. It takes a certain mind-set to either craft or appreciate the juxtapositions of wit.

Creativity. Let's define terms. Creative people are not necessarily artistic, musical or theatrical. And they are not constrained by pattern, tradition or political correctness. They're willing to imagine, to try, to risk. They're responsible for all the world's betterment (and some of its confusion, too). For some people, creativity comes out by thinking of new things to do; for others, by new ways to do them; for still others, by ways to save money, time or aggravation. Creativity is the free expression and application of a person's unique insights, talents and view of the world.

Potential. A friend tells the story of a time he was attending a conference at which Peter Drucker was a featured speaker. Someone asked Drucker if it was possible to hire potential. No, replied Drucker, potential is not measurable. Well, Drucker is technically correct. Potential may not be quantitatively measurable; however, it is qualitatively estimable. Consider this equation: Interest + Determination + Experience + Aptitude = Potential.

Hiring with potential in mind—for a select few positions for which you can afford a little slower ramp up to full capacity—is very liberating. It opens a much wider field of candidates and introduces possibilities for serendipity in your organization. Hiring someone with less than the perfect resume means that you're getting someone not as entrenched in the conventional wisdom of the field. Your "less-experienced" new hire may see with fresh eyes what a more expert candidate might overlook or dismiss. At the same time, he or she may be more willing to reject methods that no longer work no matter how well they may have worked in the past for people who "perfected" their use.

Another advantage of hiring potential—hiring someone who didn't necessarily go to the right schools or take the usual career path—is that someone you take a chance on will most likely know it. While other organizations may have discounted the abilities of the oddballs in whom you see potential,

YOU BET YOUR CAREER ON EVERY PERSON YOU HIRE.

when you hire them, they'll repay you with appreciation expressed by the desire and drive to excel in the position. (Throughout my own career, I have met people who took a risk and hired or promoted me to positions for which I was not qualified but to which I rose to the challenge through determination, hard work and, yes, gratitude.)

In considering the possibility of hiring someone for their potential, you may not necessarily hire the best qualified candidate. My colleague Ron Taddei suggests that the *right* person often makes a better fit than the *best* person.

"Done that" vs. "think that"

One of the strange twists in hiring people during the age of Radical Change is that many of the people you interview may have had excellent coaching, courtesy of an outplacement firm. In fact, your interviewees may be much better at answering employment interview questions than you are at asking them. Even without formal coaching, your candidates can come well-prepared, courtesy of a wealth of books promising to give them the magic answers to the toughest and trickiest of interview queries. Of course, glibness is no substitute for either experience or suitability, and so your job as a Value-adding Manager is to sort the "sounds good" from the "real truth." A powerful way to do that is to focus your interview questions on specific problems for which your candidate's individual solutions demonstrate a skill or competency. Detailed stories of personal actions taken to solve a problem stand in stark contrast to broad generalities ("I'm a 'people person' "), beliefs ("The customer comes first") or "we" statements ("We did this or that").

Here are some ways of focusing your nearly perfect-looking and perfect-sounding applicants on precise examples from their personal experience. These techniques give you far more meaningful insight into the job seeker than questions that spur the all-purpose generic responses (which sound more like the ideal you might want to hear rather than a nitty-gritty story from real-life incidents in the workplace).

- Can you tell me about a specific instance when you...?
- What was your personal role in that project?
- Please give me an example of how you...
- Exactly how did you...?
- What steps did you go through to...?
- Walk me through that, start to finish.
- Why did you choose that course of action?
- What alternatives did you consider?
- Who could I call to verify your example? Anyone else?

Identify high-value contributions by uncovering personal style

A story is told about Samuel Johnson, the 18th century British writer and lexicographer. A woman

179

congratulates Dr. Johnson upon publication of his *A Dictionary of the English Language* in 1755. She remarks to this great wit how grateful she was that he omitted indecent words from his thorough collection. To which he replied, "So you've been looking for them, have you, Madame?"

Moral: You find what you seek. And when you're seeking people worthy of betting your mortgage payment on, you must seek carefully. A candidate's style (his or her fundamental approach to work) is as important as specific prior experience, so you need to use interview questions that will help you uncover the real person underneath that handsome interview outfit. To get at this part of the candidate's competency, I suggest a series of interviews. Yes, it takes an investment of time at the front end, but you save far, far more on an ongoing basis.

Focus the first interview on a basic background review and evaluation of your prospective hire's technical competence. After you've established that a candidate has the requisite technical skills and experience, use subsequent conversations to assess the total person who will come to work every day. The goal is to really find out who you're about to bet your career on (and spend some significant portion of your waking hours near) before putting him or her on the payroll. You can do that through some uncommon but effective interview questions.

Note: Because these are a bit unusual, you might want to let your candidates know that you'll ask them some questions they may not have heard in other interviews. Openly address the feeling some

THE VALUE-ADDING MANAGER WANTS A STAFF THAT REPRESENTS A RICH PALETTE OF PERSPECTIVES.

candidates have that they should try to give the answer they think you want to hear. Explain that what you're trying to do is get as complete a picture of them as possible and that there are neither right answers, wrong answers, nor answers that you prefer. Invite a candid, frank and comfortable conversation. Create a warm, peer-to-peer feeling for the chat, with ample doses of humor and self-deprecation. This helps candidates relax, which is significant not because it means they will let their guards down, but because they'll reveal who they truly are: the true selves that will inevitably come out after you hire them.

- What's your favorite work you've done, even if you didn't get paid for it?
- Describe your proudest accomplishment in or out of a work environment.
- I'm sure that you're both creative and analytic. Which is your stronger quality?
- Tell me about the best boss you ever had. Why do you favor that person? And how did that affect your work?
- Tell me about the worst boss you ever had. And how did that affect your work?
- How do you know when you deliver quality?
- What have you done when people around you fail to deliver quality?
- How have you spent your past few vacations?
- What charitable or volunteer work do you do?
- What books have you read in the last year?

- Tell me about the person you admire most.
- Are you better at starting something, changing something or finishing something?
- What stands out as the greatest learning experience of your work life?
- What have you done to improve your skills in the past year?
- Tell me about a recent conflict you had with your boss.
- Can you tell me about a time when you tried to change things for the better without your boss telling you to do it?
- Tell me about a time you faced a disaster on the job.
- Imagine that sometime between two weeks and three months into this job you determine that you made a huge mistake in taking it. What would lead you to conclude that?
- If you reported to me, what would you expect from me?
- How much autonomy or supervision do you prefer?
- If given your preference, would you rather fly solo or in a group?
- Describe a work experience where things went terribly wrong. What did you do?
- Under what conditions do you do your best work?
- Tell me about a time you've been in over your head.

- I'm sure you have no shortcomings that would disqualify you for this position. But suppose I called some people who know you really well and asked them to tell me about those things that they found challenging or even disappointing about you. What would they tell me? (You might be amazed at how revealing some people are when asked this!)
- Imagine you're given a magic wand. Describe your ideal way of making a living.
- What angers you?
- Tell me about a time you made a big mistake and how it affected you.
- What do you do for fun?
- What do you feel passionate about?
- What about this position most interests you?
- What about this organization appeals to you?
- What didn't I ask you that you were expecting?
- What questions do you have for me?

Additional questions for managerial candidates

- As a boss, what are your most important responsibilities?
- Have you hired people?
- What do you look for when hiring your own staff?
- Tell me about a mistake you made in hiring.

- Have you inherited a staff in the past? How did that work out?
- Tell me about some frustrations you've had in managing others.
- Tell me about a time you needed to fire someone.
- How do you motivate people on your staff?

Look for winners' telltale signs

In your interview, certain responses, anecdotes and other clues will give you a very clear indication that you have sitting in front of you someone you want to hire. Here are some clues that turn my lights on and create an urge to make an offer on the spot:

Passion. People with strong emotions can pose more managerial challenges than those who may seem more even-keeled. The rewards are worth the risk. People of passion (for anything!) are tapped into the fullness of life. Passion is easy to detect in an interview. The candidate speaks more intently, gets excited—with joy or anger—when recounting events of personal import. The face, the whole body, expresses an unmistakable message: I care about things that happen to me and am moved to action by them. This capacity to care deeply about something often finds a connection with one's work; people who care about their work approach it vastly differently than those who don't. When you tap into this reservoir of emotion and action, you have the potential for directing a potent force for change and action.

Curiosity. People who have many questions of their own betray a wonderfully desirable characteristic: interest in the world around them. Some people are satisfied with what they're told or what they observe. For others, that limited base of information only whets their appetite for more. Those are the people I want on my staff. They're the ones who will not be satisfied with the status quo. They'll ask the questions, challenge the assumptions and pull together unrelated strands to create solutions and generate opportunities.

A healthy "we" orientation. Though I advised you earlier to dig beyond the "we-did-this-and-that" answers to your questions, some "we" answers are the best you can get, such as, "We all worked together," "It was a genuine team effort" or "I had lots of help." The ideal candidate embodies a responsibility-taking self-assurance, tempered by humility and appreciation for how others contribute to his or her success.

Gusto. Look for signs that your candidate has tried some things outside the safe lane (has taken an unusual detour on the career path, has traveled or has some broadening hobbies). Get a sense of whether this person is grounded by having had a taste of real work (maybe worked multiple jobs simultaneously, worked while going to school or did work that required getting dirty and sweaty).

Adaptability. Hire people who can likely perform in your new, unstable environment. These are

ALL BRAINS ARE GRAY, ALL BLOOD IS RED AND COMPETENCE AND GREATNESS HAVE NO COLOR, SEX OR CREED.

185

probably people who've worked for a variety of organizations or have held different posts and worked for different bosses at one workplace. They may have lived in or at least traveled to a variety of places. They may have tried starting their own business or have overcome a personal tragedy. Look for signs that the person sitting across the desk from you seeks—or at least tolerates—risk and isn't seeking a provider to guarantee care of all physical, fiscal and emotional needs.

Small-time experience. When scanning through the mountainous pile of hopeful applicants, look for work or volunteer experience with startup companies or small organizations. While a big organization may impart on its employees a useful appreciation for formal process, small ones teach an equally useful lesson: There's no such thing as "It's not my job." People who've worked in tiny shops (from hot dog stands to a Girl Scout camp), know how to multitask, pick up the slack and do whatever needs to be done.

Membership in the 2 percent club. I ask people about their volunteer or charitable experience because people who make time for such things are givers, not takers—especially if they aren't always the president of the do-gooding organization or chairman of every committee they serve on (that propensity reveals more about ego need than altruism). My wife, Susan, and I are fond of referring to the "2 percent club." Members of this unchartered organization are the people who invariably end up planning and setting up charitable events, unassumingly running them and then cleaning up afterwards without a trace of resentment or a need for recognition of their quiet heroics. We came up with the term "2 percent club" after noticing the same, very small group of people freely involved in every community or charitable organization we came in contact with. These 2-percenters do what they do because they feel a sense of purpose, their perspective pierces the merely temporal and they derive meaning and joy from giving. Can you imagine the dream job of managing an entire staff of selfless, let's-do-whatever-it-takes-to-get-the-job-done givers?

In short...

When trying to decide among good candidates, my own decision-making comes down to this simple shorthand phrase: ABCDE, which stands for Attitude, Brains, Common sense, Decency and Experience.

Of these qualities, experience receives the most attention in the usual hiring process, but it is not singularly important. It is but an element in the medley, like the noodle in your favorite pasta dish—central and indispensable but not solely sufficient. Attitude is like the sauce on the pasta; its characteristics turn the bland and generic into something unique and special. Look for can-doers, not yeah-butters.

A different view of diversity

While you'll do well to find people with a solid grounding in common sense, that isn't to suggest you hire common people. Uncommon, different, even unusual people may offer you perspective and advantages you can't find otherwise. Diversity—one of those faddish buzzwords you'd hear in management conferences—is often equated with hiring people who are ethnic minorities. Encouraging those who hold hiring power to consider all candidates certainly is in the best interest of all concerned; regrettably, some people still haven't gotten the message that all brains are gray, all blood is red and competence and greatness have no color, sex or creed.

But while it's an admirable endeavor to hire people who are not members of a majority group, it is shortsighted to limit one's view of diversity to physical characteristics or other token traits. And doing so raises odd questions: Are the women on my staff supposed to represent a female perspective? Are the black women on my staff supposed to represent either a black perspective (what is that?) or a woman's perspective? And isn't that an awful—and awfully limiting—way to think about someone's possible contribution?

Consider the questions the popular notion of diversity might raise for hiring members of one's staff: Should I give more credence to their physical characteristics, such as sex or race, than to the fact that some of them grew up speaking a language other than English? And if I do, am I not minimizing, demeaning even, their credentials (like their unique experience in other posts, graduate degrees and significant accomplishments) and their uniquely

UNCOVER THE REAL PERSON UNDERNEATH THAT HANDSOME INTERVIEW OUTFIT.

personal background? Is basing the hiring process on a set of physical characteristics like skin color or accent any better than basing it on a set like the color of one's eyes or the size of one's biceps or breasts?

True diversity—in the context of hiring—should mean striving to find people from diverse backgrounds and experiences, without concern for the origins of their gene pool. Diversity in hiring can mean employing people who are different from you and the other employees you've hired—but in ways that are less apparent than race, physical makeup or sex.

My own staff is comprised of Jewish, Gentile and other religions; Black, White and brown; male and female. It has people who grew up in cities, in suburbia and in rural areas, people who spent their whole lives in their home towns, people who moved cross-country and people who immigrated from South America and Eastern Europe. My staff includes people who worked for many large corporations and people who didn't, people who have multiple graduate degrees and people without degrees, people who have buoyant personalities and people who don't, people who like living in the city and people who detest it. Some have quick wits; others are more serious. Some are far younger than I; others, older. They are single, married, divorced, have newborns or have grandkids. One was a professional boxer (I absolutely abhor boxing but have learned much from the metaphors and sayings that he learned in his years in the gym); another is an amateur actor; another does fund raising for her

189

alma mater. There are all kinds in this group of fewer than 20.

Interestingly, some who are far different from me physically are actually much more similar to me psychically. So if someone were lumping my staff into categories based on characteristics like race and sex, they'd group us all wrong. While I value the apparent diversity of my group, I value their competence and their values more than that. For as different as we all are physically, we share many traits that really count: mutual respect, dedication to excellence and a commitment to working together to do what needs to be done.

Only fools deny employment opportunities to people because they belong to a physically identifiable group. Anyone who does does it at the risk of lacking the insight or range of experience necessary to meet the challenges thrown their way by Radical Change or business as usual. The Value-adding Manager wants the best people and a staff that represents not a homogenous perspective but a rich palette of perspectives. The Value-adding Manager pursues diversity, not to be politically correct or to engage in social engineering, but because this is the way to ensure a rich pool of perspectives, insights and fresh thinking. Sometimes having this goal in mind means choosing people who may not be the candidates with the strongest technical skills or backgrounds. But technical skills are the easiest to come by; books, courses and a helpful mentor can develop most any of them in relatively short order.

The other attributes are formed during a lifetime, are unique and are not interchangeable.

Radical hiring practices

Some might suggest that the advice in this chapter on hiring people is radical. And they'd be right. The origin of the word "radical" is a Latin word meaning "having roots." And that is precisely what I'm suggesting you keep in mind when evaluating and trying to choose among people: What are their roots? Are they rooted in an ethical system that will encourage them to do all the right things (which you might define many different ways)? Are they rooted in diverse experiences in a variety of places that will help them help your organization by virtue of their fresh insights? Are they rooted in self-assurance, a medley of skills and a desire to learn constantly so that they'll adapt and triumph regardless of the challenge?

And most importantly, are you rooted sufficiently in your good judgment to take a chance on people who may not have been fired in the customary mold but whose bright light and burning desire offer your organization the prospect of brilliant achievements?

Chapter 10

Staying sane while going crazy: Leader as well-adjusted human being

The rigors of Radical Change test you like nothing else. In its grip, you'll work longer hours, handle more challenges and make more decisions than you thought possible. Adrenaline will become your best friend. A good night's sleep may become slightly less familiar.

Radical Change's constant barrage of new demands can be simultaneously invigorating and exhausting. How you manage your own response to the unbelievable expectations you face will have everything to do with how long and how well you endure. When Radical Change crashes into your life, you must master it or it will master you. Doing that may be as simple as adjusting your perspective on it. You know it's not going away and that you can't undo its effects. So the key is to see it as an instrument of your personal growth, as the springboard from which you leap to the next level in your career. You

WHAT MATTERS MOST IN LIFE DOESN'T HAPPEN AT THE OFFICE.

193

can view the work it dumps on your lap as an obligation or as stimulation.

Naive? No. Think of it this way: Sometimes people refer to challenges as hurdles, and some people
run real hurdles on purpose—for the sport and
challenge of the exercise. That's the way to view the
hurdles put in your career track by Radical Change.
Sure, they're too high and too close for comfort. So
you need to get better at clearing some, avoiding
others and knocking others aside. Remember,
Radical Change changes the game, so you get to
reinvent how you run the hurdles. The most important thing is to lace up, psyche up and go for it.
Nearly impossible hard work, approached with the
right attitude, can be fun (or at least not miserable).
I like to think of the mental condition created by the
onslaught of challenges as being high on stress.

Here are some ways you can help yourself cope
with your overwhelming agenda.

Hire smart; manage tough. Chapter 9 went into
detail about hiring the right people. That's helpful
advice for building a better staff when you have
openings, but maybe you have no vacancies following the purge forced by Radical Change. Maybe you
need to create some. Look, the truth of the matter is
that you assembled a staff to do certain tasks in a
pre-Radical Change environment. The work you
originally hired people to do may not exist anymore.
You hired square pegs for your square holes—a good
fit. Since that time, some of those square holes have
been recut to round holes, and the fit is gone. To ask

your square pegs to break their backs trying to fit into round holes isn't doing them a favor.

Admitting that your fine square pegs aren't suitable for your round holes is not a condemnation of them or you. It only recognizes the difference created by a reality you didn't design and couldn't foresee. When you stop trying to force really fine square peg staffers to complete the impossible mission of filling those round holes, the terrible stress on everyone is relieved.

Give yourself and your key people a promotion: Redistribute work. Staying on top of a tremendous increase in your responsibility in the wake of Radical Change probably means giving some of your work to your staff. And the work you may shift to them could very well be work that you personally enjoy doing. In the past couple of years, I've handed staffers work that I loved. Like keeping order in our closets, sometimes we have to give up some favorite things that don't fit to make room for new things.

In the process, you get a chance to tackle new responsibilities—a growth experience—and so do members of your staff. It's like everyone's getting a promotion to new duties (paid more in mental paychecks than fiscal). The kind of person I am and the kind of people I try to hire welcome growth—even the kind forced by circumstance.

Today's high-tech management tools both compress and expand time and work. Voice mail, electronic mail, fax machines, portable phones, laptop and palmtop computers, pagers—these all promise to help you work more efficiently, both in the office and at home. These devices *can* make you more productive—and *less* productive.

With the technology my employer has put at my disposal both in my office and in my home, I am now fully capable of working 24 hours a day every day of the year. I leave the office late, only to go home and dial into my phone mail; I find messages that I reply to. Then I sit down at the computer and dial into the e-mail system I just left at the office and find new messages. While I'm on vacation, I get faxes at home or in my hotel; the express delivery truck follows me virtually everywhere I go. Technology now means that there is no escape from work. The pundits who were musing just a few years back about the end to the 40-hour workweek were half right. It ended all right, but it didn't turn into the 30-hour week some predicted. The dirty little secret about productivity-enhancers is that fewer people can now do more work.

I have and use just about every electronic productivity device there is. And yes, I'm darn productive. I personally oversee operations that four times as many managers once did (and no, I don't draw anywhere near their collective salaries). So I'm a good bargain for my employer and good for our stockholders. While I'm now capable of working every minute of every day even if I'm thousands of miles away from the office, I try not to. Even the best and most durable machines need "downtime" for maintenance and repair. Super managers are no different. You'll do better work when you're rested

THINK OF THE MENTAL CONDITION CREATED BY THE ONSLAUGHT OF CHALLENGES AS BEING HIGH ON STRESS.

than when you're suffering from sleep deprivation. You'll do better work when you can focus and concentrate than when you're burned out.

Idle a little. Some people fall into a terrible trap of self-delusion. They believe, "I'm busy so I must be valuable." It's easy to conclude that. After all, the word "business" comes from "busy-ness." But busyness has no value at all; *results* count. So stop equating the volume of your activities with your intrinsic worth. Ignore some voice mail, e-mail, faxes and written messages. Technology has vastly increased the capacity for nearly everyone to inundate you with great volumes of useless distractions. Being polite and responsive can kill your productivity and maybe endanger your health. Let some things go; the business won't come crashing down. (Refer back to Chapter 6 for some suggestions on prioritizing your work.)

Stay interested in and excited by what you do. If you begin to find your job boring, either create some excitement...or leave. If you're bored, your people won't be excited either. Soon, the whole operation will slip into mediocrity or worse, and then your employer will solve your boredom problem in a dramatic and final way. To rekindle your enthusiasm, get to an industry or professional conference (even if you have to pay for it out of personal funds) and find out what others like you are doing. Call your counterparts at other companies to swap stories. Read the latest book in your field; see what new knowledge you might apply or techniques you might try. Get away; take as long a vacation as you can away from the din that deadened your interest. When you return, refreshed and renewed, the old place probably will look pretty good again. If it doesn't, start looking for a new place to ply your craft.

Pursue the golden mean

Reality check: What matters most in life doesn't happen at the office. Many who'd agree with this truth unfortunately don't live their lives in harmony with it. But understanding that the office is but a part of life makes you more effective there. You'll approach issues with a broader perspective, not myopia. Woody Allen said that no one on their deathbed looks back wishing they'd worked harder. Strive to make your work life a balanced part of a total life.

When people lose touch with work's proper place in life, they suffer physically (eating, drinking or smoking too much, creating or aggravating an ulcer or other manifestations of stress gone amuck). Stress is self-inflicted. Sure, there are important consequences riding on what you do at the office, but none is worth risking your health. Stop and remind yourself of that. When work threatens to smother you, to squeeze the very best from you, take a walk. Clear your head.

When you're under pressure, you might find solace in food and find no time to burn off even modestly excessive calories. You face a choice: Extra size or exercise? Moderation on your plate and moderate exercise both contribute to your success; you feel better physically and psychologically, and because you do, you'll perform better managerially. When Radical Change consumes virtually every waking hour, there doesn't seem to be much time to dedicate to formal exercise programs. Still, there are little ways to sneak little life-giving physical workouts into even a jam-packed day. The easiest is simply to walk more. I intentionally park far away from the train station from which I commute every day to force myself to walk farther than I have to. The extra six minutes it adds coming and going don't make an appreciable dent in my intense schedule, but they do help me get the blood going in the morning and aid a wind-down in the evening. In the meantime, I take steps, not elevators or escalators, whenever possible. I make a point of walking the long way to someone's office or a conference room. When meetings break for coffee, I use every moment I can to walk the hall-ways (not only do I stretch my legs, I get a chance to at least say hello to people I might not otherwise even see for days at a time). While I used to take lunch at my desk quite often, I now avoid that as much as possible, opting instead for a quick walk out-side for a change of scenery, a little leg stretching and some fresh air. This little excursion makes the afternoon more productive (because I'm fresher) than if I had never unchained myself from the desk.

While every weekend could be spent nonstop on work, it shouldn't. Diversions give you a chance to climb out of the work rut, to clear the week's cob-webs for a better view come Monday. For a few years, I became so engaged in nothing but the obligations of work and child-rearing that I literally did nothing for myself. I lost interest in the job and found its challenges not only uninvigorating but downright annoying. But then I decided to rekindle an old hobby, outdoor photography. To free up time for that, I gave up a set of chores I never liked anyway—lawn care (which I entrusted to my teenage son and professionals). Upon rediscovering my long-lost friend the camera and the environs it took me to (frequently with one of my kids), I found sanity returning at a rapid rate. When I climbed back into the saddle on Monday morning, I was refreshed—not more exhausted than when I dragged myself home on Friday. If you long to do some woodworking, needlepoint, working out at the gym or whatever, give permission to yourself to find a way to do it—it's an investment in your productivity!

An easy way to escape from the office, even when you're forced to stay right there, is to always have a vacation scheduled. Knowing that there's an exit up ahead makes the long stretch of bad road more endurable. Some vacations can be as simple as a three-day weekend. (I suggest taking off Monday, not Friday; when Monday rolls around, you'll already be more relaxed and get more out of your day off than you might if you had prematurely ended your go-go-go week a day early.) If your plan calls for going someplace or at least doing something fun, it provides you with an instantly available daydream escape. Just close your eyes and imagine yourself there and not where you are. A pleasant future makes the present more endurable.

Another way to add balance to your work life is to have a wider social circle than the corporate one. If you're mostly socializing with people from the shop—no matter how much you like them as individuals—you're limiting your outlook. People from other walks of life may have challenges similar to those you face at work, but they have other experiences and insights to offer you. The pleasure of their company offers you diversion from work and, in the process, may help you be more effective when you return there.

An article on performance management in my employer's company newsletter quoted this wonderful goal from one of our employees: "Have more fun. Get control of my schedule so that I have more heart and soul to throw into my work, and into the rest of my life." Exactly.

Me, Inc.

"I gave the best years of my life to that company." This retort is commonly heard from bitter former employees. You should avoid ever being in a position to say this sentiment of regret. All the way through your employment, you should be feeling that there is a fair relationship between what you're giving your employer and what you're getting in return. That way, if the relationship were to end abruptly, you wouldn't feel cheated or abused (though you might well feel saddened).

STOP EQUATING THE VOLUME OF YOUR ACTIVITIES WITH YOUR INTRINSIC WORTH.

If you're at a company primarily because you hope that someday it will repay you for your current investment of time and effort, you are speculating and setting yourself up for disappointment. In the age of Radical Change, you are selling skills and your employer is buying them. Nothing more is implied in the employment relationship. It is willing seller, willing buyer. If you believe it's anything other than that, prepare for disappointment, and immediately begin working toward a better arrangement than the one you're in now.

It may be hard to think of offering your skills to another organization, either because you've been at your current employer for so long or because you so strongly identify yourself with it. Identity with one's employer is something companies have encouraged for decades by printing their logos on clothing, pens, mugs, jewelry and just about anything that can be imprinted or affixed with the hallowed corporate seal. Even as the so-called social contract between employer and employee is being redefined, the notion of an organization's imprinting itself on its employees' souls is slow to die. Take, for example, this excerpt from a recent article in a human resources magazine written by (of all people) a senior vice president of a major outplacement firm: "The employer provides security, in the form of a paycheck, benefits and *identity* [emphasis added]; in return, employees give back attendance, loyalty and dedication."

Taking your identity from your job or the organization that pays you to hold it denies you control over it. Your identity does not and should not come from your employer. You are a skilled professional who is responsible for your own career, and you may find that that career takes you to many different payrolls. But on each of them, you retain the rights to your identity.

In the "Me, Incorporated" way of operating, your career is your own unique set of ever-growing skills and experiences, not the succession of positions within one organization.

The very term "job security" is probably one that will soon drop from common usage. It will be replaced by a different concept: income security, which comes not from an employer but rather from your own marketable skills. The importance of making the transition to this concept grows every day; the U.S. Bureau of Labor Statistics reports that the median tenure of employees at a company is only 4.5 years and shrinking.

One way to help ensure that you have marketable skills is to make a point of doing resume-quality work. As you endeavor to add value to your current organization, try doing things your next one will appreciate just as much. Or more.

Invest in yourself

Dealing with the complex mess created by Radical Change leaves little time for reading newspapers or trade and professional journals. In trying to stay even with the challenges of the day, it's easy to let slide your preparation for those you'll face tomorrow.

But to stay sharp and competitive, make time, on vacation if necessary, to at least skim some appropriate magazines and books. You probably can't take the time you once did for professional reading, but you certainly can't stop doing it altogether (if you want to stay employable).

As you're working to keep your professional knowledge current, prepare for a "personal reengineering." This means constantly reevaluating your work expectations against what you consider sufficiently rewarding compensation (expect increasing amounts of risk and much less frequent increases to base salary). It also means upgrading and finetuning your skills.

ALWAYS HAVE
A VACATION
SCHEDULED.

Another way to both lower your stress level and secure your fiscal peace of mind is to save and invest some cash. You can give yourself a safety net with a disciplined set-aside program by which you automatically invest some piece of your regular paycheck in a money market account or mutual fund. Having this little extra fiscal security goes a long way toward shoring up your psychological security when you're buffeted by the threatening storms of Radical Change.

Develop the 10 competencies of leadership

All the techniques, procedures and methods you can muster aren't enough to succeed in leading others through troubled waters. Methods, no matter how intricate or sophisticated, are at some level a variation on "insert tab A into slot B." Effective leadership emanates from a deeper reservoir. Here are 10 competencies that effective leaders work to develop; they have less to do with what you do and everything to do with who you're becoming.

1. Clarity of purpose. If you would presume to lead others, know where you want to take them. Understand what drives you to do what you do. Knowing why is as important as knowing how.

2. Initiative. Leaders are starters and agenda-setters. When you lead, things happen and people move because you start them.

3. Results imperative. Leaders embody a firm resolve to a defined end and inspire others to reach it. As a true leader, you impart a sense of mission in your colleagues by your own desire to reach the defined destination.

4. Persuasive authority. Effective leaders communicate in a compelling way. Some quietly, some boldly, all unmistakably clearly. People will follow you when they understand where you would take them.

5. Equilibrium. The best leaders are complete people with balance in their lives. When you have a full life, you are rewarded with a broad perspective and better judgment.

6. Perpetual learner. Leaders possess some technical knowledge—knowing something about something. While you don't need to know more than those you lead, you must understand what they're dealing with. Leaders know what they don't know, and they know they always benefit from knowing more.

7. Commitment to quality, in all of life. Leaders inspire (and sometimes push) others to achieve great things. As a leader, you serve as an example for seeking excellence (but not perfection) in everything you do.

8. Open mind. Leaders willingly consider alternatives, accept the validity of ideas even if they are unfamiliar and are not bound by convention, tradition or the prevailing opinion.

9. Ethic of service. Leadership carries a set of responsibilities and accountabilities and requires making difficult decisions. Nothing in any of those obligations suggests you possess membership in an elite class. You don't. Leadership is a privilege.

10. Compassion. The term literally means "to suffer with another." Leaders understand and empathize with those they'd presume to lead and understand the costs they ask others to bear. You can touch people most deeply when they feel your humanity.

Conclusion

Loyalty, tenure and disposability: Reflections on corporate downsizing

"The very term 'corporate loyalty' has an archaic ring to it. Indeed, loyalty to a company is considered by many a betrayal of self."

—Alvin Toffler, author, *The Third Wave*

"People's occupation is theirs to take with them . . . Their employer may have given it to them but can't take it away."

—Srully Blotnik, psychologist

It's easy to deride the corporate rage for paring the payroll. Studies and surveys report that many—perhaps most—efforts to skinny-up the bloated

WORKERS ON A PAYROLL HAVE BEEN SHIELDED FOR YEARS FROM REALITY AS MANY OTHERS KNOW IT.

corporate corpus have no lasting positive effect. But it's also clear that technology and pervasive global competition are coconspirators in a major social and economic upheaval, the shock waves of which have been as devastating to many as if their homes had been hit by a tornado. (Metaphors of death and execution accompany talk of job eliminations for a reason.)

While it may not be difficult to find corporations that shortsightedly threw employees out of their jobs for a quick reduction in costs and a short-lived boost in profit ("dumbsizing"), more than quick-fix greed is at work here. The Episcopal Church grabbed headlines when it announced in September of 1994 that it was struggling to reduce its administrative costs and would lay off staff at its New York headquarters. While budget pressures turned attention most immediately to pink slips for administrative staff, church officials were also examining the very principles underlying the church's structure (how many houses of delegates, how many regional officials to preside over church affairs, how often national conferences are held, how much emphasis was put on national activism or local involvement). Such an endeavor by church leaders speaks to the very principles of reengineering—the popular concept by which an organization sets out to virtually reinvent itself by identifying every assumption behind every operation, questioning every assumption and perhaps changing most every operation.

Many organizations, like the Episcopal Church, undertake painful self-examination and tighten their belts when financial troubles necessitate it. But a growing number of major corporations are going through the "shave costs" drill when they're quite fiscally healthy (much the same way one might prune a healthy plant to help improve future growth). Working for even a reasonably profitable and stable organization is no hedge against the unemployment line. That's why, in each of several recent years, many hundreds of thousands of otherwise gainfully employed people joined the ranks of the jobless. Continuous employment is tenuous.

The lowdown costs of high-tech savings

Today's pervasive computers, smart automation systems and high-tech office equipment are as threatening to many workers as the steam drill was to John Henry. Technology improves productivity, but, as stated earlier, the dirty little secret about productivity improvements is the need for fewer human workers. Unlike previous technological improvements, such as the replacement of the manual typewriter with the electric one, today's advances mean fewer people need show up for work to get the job done. Personal computers and voice mail systems mean not only fewer secretaries and receptionists but fewer managers to handle and relay information throughout an organization. Improved manufacturing technology means not only making more precise and higher quality products but producing more output per manufacturing employee. Highly productive organizations are increasingly putting out more work with increasingly less labor.

It's tempting to paint a picture of capitalists as contemptible opportunists who eagerly trade a tool for a worker, but isn't that what capitalists are supposed to do? A healthy enterprise gets that way by meeting a need in the market and doing it efficiently. Today's new technology is merely a flashier descendent of a long lineage of inventions dating back to the cotton gin, the iron horse, the Model T and so on. Should we fault plumbers for the precipitous fall in the number of people employed as outhouse constructors?

American workers find fault with their organizations when they don't imply an assurance of uninterrupted employment. The notion has few corollaries in our society. The farmer up the road has no assurance the corn won't suffer severe damage in a storm this summer. The video rental store down the street has no guarantee that another, fancier video store won't move in two doors down or that some new inexpensive satellite or broadcast medium won't entirely displace the store's very reason for being. The dry cleaner down the block has no protection from a fashion trend of wearing fewer dry-clean-only suits and more casual, machine washable clothing to the office.

Workers on a payroll have been shielded for years from reality as many others know it. They were

"JOB SECURITY" ISN'T QUITE AN OXYMORON, BUT IT IS A QUAINT IDEA WHOSE BETER DAYS ARE BEHIND US.

spoiled by the post-World War II presumption that if manufacturers produced goods, someone somewhere in the world would buy them. For decades producers produced, buyers bought and employees were employed. The postwar economy gave way to a new order in a new world with new (and fewer) constants, less margin to fund programs, fewer entitlements and a bureaucracy that seems less tolerable than it was in the good old days.

Employees can argue that they, unlike the farmer, the store owner and other small business owners, are uniquely vulnerable to unemployment because their livelihood comes from a sole primary source—a single employer—and is not spread across a wide base of customers. However, unlike the farmer, the store owner and other small business owners, employees don't have to take out loans or a second mortgage on their homes to invest in a business just so they can enjoy the privilege of trying to make a living—a privilege that is uncertain and carries the risk of financial ruin.

So, as callous as the new corporate way is—employed today but maybe not tomorrow—it reflects a purer, more realistic form of capitalism. It also raises troubling questions for everyone while the whole of society catches up to the new employment reality. More and more corporate employees, both former and current, are realizing that the benevolent corporation no longer can be counted on to provide workers with benefits such as health and life insurance. The kindly and expensive generosity that companies provide their employees can turn into an ugly, horrific tragedy. Shortly after being expatriated from the payroll, employees face the prospect of no or very expensive health insurance at the very time when they may be least equipped to deal with that change. For many employees, much of their social and health support system is tightly intertwined with their (now former) employer.

To talk about the emerging "free agent" model in which people sell their full-time labor to organizations is one thing. It's quite another to reconcile the disparity in most people's readiness for the implications of that change. Employers need to clearly and overtly communicate to workers about the change in their relationship and be forthcoming about all the risks the individual now faces (and probably always did, but the problem seemed less serious with ample employment opportunities for displaced workers).

So what about loyalty?

In 1990, the management consulting firm Booz-Allen & Hamilton released a study entitled "Job Security: A Forecast." A vice president of the firm told the *New York Times*, "We believe that job security will increase in the 1990s, and that represents a reversal of a trend of the past 15 years. . . . We see that companies have begun to recognize [that] the next wave of productivity involves the improvement of employee effectiveness, not just cost reductions from further downsizing." The consultant predicted that in five years corporations would change their attitudes and once again embrace job security and offer lifetime employment. "I think management is beginning to appreciate greater loyalty from the value standpoint," he observed.

It's both unfair and far too easy to ridicule such an off-base, near-term prediction of the corporate landscape by a most respected management consulting firm. The inaccuracy does, however, point to the tenuous nature of Corporate America's attitude toward assuring continuing employment for its workers (not to mention the extraordinary irony that Booz-Allen & Hamilton has since become quite renowned for its role in designing downsizings).

The popular notion of loyalty, the one contemplated in the Booz-Allen study, is oddly contorted. Many use the term "loyalty" as nearly interchangeable with "blind, undying devotion." Some employees expect their employer to show them greater and longer lasting commitment than their spouses or parents. Likewise, some business managers expect or demand that employees sacrifice nearly all else in order to stay (temporarily) on the payroll, extracting more fidelity than most marriages enjoy. "Loyalty" comes from the same root as the word for legal. Someone who is loyal makes good on his or her commitments and faithfully discharges his or her duty. In other words, a loyal employee provides an honest day's work for an honest day's pay. A colleague raised in the South relates advice her mother gave her decades ago, "The company ain't your daddy!" It ain't neither your mama nor your friend.

SOMEONE WHO IS LOYAL MAKES GOOD ON HIS OR HER COMMITMENTS AND FAITHFULLY DISCHARGES HIS OR HER DUTY.

213

It's an abstract, unfeeling, self-serving entity that purchases services from you for only as long as it chooses. The game is willing seller, willing buyer. Each has legal obligations to the other. When those obligations have been faithfully fulfilled, each can be said to have been loyal.

Loyalty, in the strict sense of the word, may not be out of favor but rather redefined in terms of its time span. An employing organization and its skill providers might deal with one another with integrity, honesty, mutual respect and loyalty—but without expectations for a never-ending relationship. With fewer employees, more and more companies are getting work done not through full-time staff but through itinerant nonemployees. Contract services, consultants, freelancers, part-time and temporary employees are all the rage. And why shouldn't they be? Corporations and other organizations exist to provide goods or services to those who value them. Employing people is a part of, but not central to, that mission (and certainly issuing health, dental and vision insurance, legal services and the like are at best peripheral to it). Many people who've left the traditional corporate fold have found their way (either by choice or necessity) into the "for temporary hire" category. Whether corporations find in the long run that putting resources to work on a nonexclusive and occasional basis can provide the same or better service as their former full-time employee counterparts remains to be seen.

One thing's certain: In today's business environment, the term "job security" isn't quite an oxymoron, but it *is* a quaint idea whose better days are behind us. Rather than lamenting about what is no more, the wise will get about the work of embracing what is and preparing for what will be.

About the author

Don Blohowiak is a marketing executive in a successfully downsized, and very profitable, unit of the Times Mirror Co. Now based in New York City, he has held management posts in Southern California, Denver, Detroit and Milwaukee. Every day he encounters the pressures, challenges and opportunities of Radical Change.

This book is his fourth. His previous works include: *Lead Your Staff to Think Like Einstein, Create Like da Vinci, and Invent Like Edison* (Irwin Professional Publishing, 1995), *Mavericks!* (Business One Irwin, 1992), *No Comment! An Executive's Essential Guide to the News Media* (Praeger, 1987).

Widely interviewed and quoted by the major print and broadcast news media, Don is also a provocative and entertaining public speaker. He counts many associations and corporations as speaking clients, including Prudential Insurance, Dow Jones and Exxon. He is represented by JR Associates in Princeton, NJ (609-921-6605).

You can contact Don at:

Box 791
Princeton Junction, NJ 08550-0791
Internet: 76016.1446@compuserve.com.

Index